# UNDER ESTIMATED

# UNDER ESTIMATED

CHELSEY GOODAN

## THE WISDOM AND POWER OF TEENAGE GIRLS

G

GALLERY BOOKS

NEW YORK   LONDON   TORONTO   SYDNEY   NEW DELHI

# G

Gallery Books
An Imprint of Simon & Schuster, LLC.
1230 Avenue of the Americas
New York, NY 10020

First Gallery Books hardcover edition March 2024

GALLERY BOOKS and colophon are registered trademarks of Simon & Schuster, LLC.

Simon & Schuster: Celebrating 100 Years of Publishing in 2024

For information about special discounts for bulk purchases, please contact Simon & Schuster Special Sales at 1-866-506-1949 or business@simonandschuster.com.

The Simon & Schuster Speakers Bureau can bring authors to your live event. For more information or to book an event, contact the Simon & Schuster Speakers Bureau at 1-866-248-3049 or visit our website at www.simonspeakers.com.

Interior design by Davina Mock-Maniscalco
Feelings Wheel design by Laura Levatino

Manufactured in the United States of America

10  9  8  7  6  5  4  3  2  1

Library of Congress Cataloging-in-Publication Data

Names: Goodan, Chelsey, author.
Title: Underestimated : the wisdom and power of teenage girls / Chelsey Goodan.
Description: First Gallery Books hardcover edition. | New York : Gallery Books, 2024.
Identifiers: LCCN 2023042576 (print) | LCCN 2023042577 (ebook) |
    ISBN 9781668032688 (hardcover) | ISBN 9781668032701 (ebook)
Subjects: LCSH: Teenage girls.
Classification: LCC HQ798 .G663 2024 (print) | LCC HQ798 (ebook) |
    DDC 305.235/2—dc23/eng/20231213
LC record available at https://lccn.loc.gov/2023042576
LC ebook record available at https://lccn.loc.gov/2023042577

ISBN 978-1-6680-3268-8
ISBN 978-1-6680-3270-1 (ebook)

*I dedicate this book to all the girls who profoundly expanded my mind and heart, helping to heal the teenage girl inside of me.*

## AUTHOR'S NOTE

To respect the privacy of the teenage girls who shared their thoughts and stories with me, I have changed names and some identifying details, and in some instances, I created composites due to the commonality of their stories.

But also know, a lot of teenage girls read, edited, and consulted on this book during the entire process, holding me accountable to their most honest, collective truth.

# CONTENTS

"I want to inform them that I am not silent because I have nothing to say. I am silent because nobody is listening."[1]

KELSEY SUTTON

# (FEAR)

Teenage girls want to scream. A cathartic, stunning, determined, relentless scream. A transformative scream that tears down emotional walls and connects to what's true. A battle cry loud enough to shatter the glass above her and obliterate what tries to contain her. A scream that requires everyone to listen, *really* listen.

It's not the scream of annoyance that we hear in moments of her exasperation. Rather an earth-shaking scream that emerges from her own exquisite power. A scream we aren't hearing because it's trapped inside, stifled by a world that fears teenage girls.

A fear that silences them.

They're dismissed as "hormonal," "crazy," and "dramatic," which minimizes their voice until it's silent. The narrative of fear has become so normalized that we don't even question it. The examples are so easy to draw from because they're still so commonplace and familiar:

Expectant parents who are relieved that they're having a boy because they've heard about the terror and emotional lawlessness of a teenage girl.

Mothers who remember how much they fought with their own

moms and who are now scared of being hated by their own teenage girl.

Fathers who worry about defending their little girl from male suitors, forcefully trying to control her choices.

Schools fearing the way teenage girls dress, inventing rules to ensure their "modesty."

Adults scared of the sexuality that fills teenage girls' social media feeds, harshly judging them with labels of "shallow," "too sexy," and "irresponsible."

Cliché? Sure. But also, very much the prevailing way our society stereotypes teenage girls. This fear seeps into our own insecurities, knowing that a teenage girl has the ability to rip us apart at any moment with her cutting, perceptive words. Even if you're a person who likes to encourage and support teenage girls, it's still easy to succumb to our societal fear of her vocal, emotional, and sexual potential. It's much easier to hide behind walls of misunderstanding and avoidance. Because if we look honestly . . . we'll see a teenage girl's vast and electric *power*.

A power that has been bound up, warped, and restrained because people don't know what to do with it. They don't know how to connect to it. Out of that fear and lack of understanding, we squash the liberated, fierce, passionate spirit right out of that bright, smiling, limitless face, until she's consumed by "perfection" and pleasing others. Until she's lost in a blur of teenage angst. We squash—and consequently, I've come to learn, over years of working closely with teenage girls— we've been squashing a wildly underestimated force for good in the world.

---

For the last 16 years, I've had the great honor of being welcomed into a rarefied space—having earned the trust of teenage girls. As a private tutor and mentor, I get hours upon hours of concentrated, intimate, and depth-filled conversation covering the topics in her brain. This is the brain I want to welcome everyone into, loudly proclaiming at the entrance: "Not Shallow. Only for Swimmers who can handle the Deep End." Her brain is filled with questions and thoughts on relationships, world history, sexism, self-confidence, psychology, grades, eating disorders, social media, math, racism, love, birth control, literature, resilience, colonialism, body image, chemistry, TV, social justice, grammar, boys, finances, God, teachers, sports, queer identities, college, self-compassion, celebrities, Spanish, anxiety, sex, climate change, spelling, feminism, emotions, tests, fashion, biology, stress, ethics, parents, sexual assault, movies, politics, rejection, careers, mental health, volunteering, bullying, perfectionism, or one of the other eight million things going through her mind.

We talk endlessly with each other because it's an incredibly special and safe space where I invite a teenage girl to be her full self. With me, she can be that girl who wants to scream because I tell her that I still have that girl inside of me too.

I've become the person who she texts at 10 p.m. overwhelmed with anxiety and needing encouragement. Sharing with me both her stress while sobbing and her wins during a celebratory meal, she knows I'm the person who *believes* her and believes *in* her. I'm the person who brings over Krispy Kreme donuts to celebrate her coming out to her friends. I'm the person who agrees that Timothée Chalamet is a national treasure and who will happily dissect the love triangles that saturate teenagers' favorite TV shows. We'll also read a summer book together for fun and go on hikes to discuss it. Her family will often invite me into meaningful moments, sitting in the "family section" at a bat mitzvah or being asked to officiate her wedding someday. Without encroaching on the vital role of a parent, I create a relationship with teenage girls that carries a tone of ease and care, which grows out of sharing so much of our lives together.

A huge priority with this book is to hand the microphone over to the voices of teenage girls so that we all can hear them and listen to them. These girls have taught me more than I've ever taught them. I've been in some very difficult trenches with them, and the lessons I've learned are for *everyone*. If you have a teenage girl in your life, I promise that after reading this book you will learn how to better understand, connect with, and support her. And if you don't have a teenage girl in your life, I promise you will personally heal and grow from the lessons that these girls vulnerably share here. *They represent the change we're all yearning for and also the fear that holds us back.*

*Underestimated* is informed by thousands of hours spent with over a hundred teenage girls, varying in socioeconomic status, ability, location, sexual orientation, religion, cultural background, and about half of them identifying as not white. The topic of each chapter was chosen by girls telling me their specific struggles. Each chapter then reveals the inspiring lessons these girls have taught me around that specific struggle. I've found that the solution to a teenage girl's well-being lies within her—she just needs someone to believe in her power to discover it.

So many books refer to teenage girls with a top-down mentality, where the power lies with the adult, advising parents on how to get their daughter to do what they want. In contrast, we're going to ask the teenage girl what she wants. I'm hoping you'll be pleasantly surprised by the rewards this brings. I'm asking you to expect the unexpected. These girls are offering a *new* path forward for all of us.

*Underestimated* is an intimate, gutsy dive into the Deep End. A place that's largely unexplored. Fifteen-year-old Waverly couldn't hold back her excitement to share her experiences, and as a flood of deep thoughts poured out of her, she declared:

"I've been waiting my whole life to be asked these questions!"

Teenage girls love to be asked smart, pointed questions. Not questions with a secret agenda, not questions trying to bond with them, not generalized questions like "How is school?" They like questions relating to their honest thoughts on the type of topics specified by *Underestimated*'s chapter titles. Interestingly, when I told teenage girls

I was writing this book, many of them exclaimed, "Oh good, because you actually understand me!!"

I've learned that *teenage girls feel profoundly misunderstood* all the time. This sparked my question for all of them:

"If there was one thing you wished that adults understood about teenage girls, what would it be?"

The resounding answer was:

*"We're a lot smarter than you think we are."*

When I asked sixteen-year-old Peeta, who didn't answer with that response right away, she rolled her eyes and said, "Oh, well, that's just too obvious. Of course we're smarter than they think. Honestly, there are soooo many things I wish they'd understand better. Like everything."

That was another popular answer: *"Everything."*

By revealing many of their mysteries in this book, I'm hoping to change the status quo of how teenage girls are viewed, because they thrive when they feel understood. This feeling strengthens them to step into their own happiness, wholeness, and power.

When I tell parents that I get teenage girls to open up, to be vulnerable and share, they furrow their brow in disbelief:

"How do you do that?" "She doesn't want to talk to me!" "She's mean." "She won't listen!" "She's too cool for me." "She's so emotional." "She snaps at me!" "I don't know why she hates me!"

I hear you, and I'm going to help.

Maybe you've picked this book up because you're having difficulty connecting with or relating to your daughter. In these pages, I share ways to create a clean slate, so that a deeper connection can be made between you. Having had so many parents ask me how to talk to their daughters, it inspired me to actually provide you with the words, questions, and comments that will impact her most.

And because I love efficiency, I've included five core insights at the end of each chapter and a guide in Appendix 2 that explicitly gives you words to expand conversations to develop connections not only with teenage girls but also with yourself and others.

Rather than teenage girls rolling their eyes at your questions, I'm offering you the language that will expand your conversations in a way that allows more admiration and respect to flow into your relationship. I'm also going to model how to sincerely communicate with a tone that a girl can hear and take in. And as a result, she won't feel so misunderstood. She will feel seen and heard.

And when that happens, she's straight-up going to like you more. And you're going to like her more.

That's when it gets really fun. I'm going to bring you into the magic that happens when a teenage girl feels safe to be her authentic self. It's a space filled with ups and downs, and *so much love.*

My relationship with teenage girls is different than that of a teacher or therapist because it's a different type of intimacy that doesn't require any type of judgment or evaluation. My insights are not clinical or academic, but rather they come from a long-term mentorship that connects with a teenage girl several times a week—in person or by FaceTime, text, voice note, Instagram DMs, or (gasp!) an old-fashioned phone call. I've been in the homes of incredibly influential families while also volunteering my time to work with girls from underserved communities, and most recently as the mentorship director of the nonprofit DemocraShe, a nationwide program that encourages and guides high school girls from diverse backgrounds into leadership roles.

When I mention parents in these pages, please know that my regard for them is filled with so much compassion, love, and respect. I feel profoundly honored by and grateful for the trust that parents have given me in supporting their daughters. I myself am not a parent, which I have to admit has definitely helped me enter territory where parents are oftentimes denied access. Girls have told me that it's easier to admit their mistakes to me because they feel no pressure, judgment, or "parental vibes" from me, which helps create an environment where they feel safe to be incredibly honest. I've filled a different role in a teenage girl's life that's definitely not as difficult or complicated as a parent's. Thankfully, it has offered me an inside look into a girl's very human, universal struggles, allowing me to experience her full spectrum of wisdom.

Wisdom? Yes. We often think that age or experience is the main barometer of wisdom. Time offers significant lessons, but historically, we do not listen to our youth, even though they have always led the charge for progress. From the protests of the Vietnam War to the efforts to combat climate change today, our youth have been shouting for our attention. Instead, we dismiss them as young, thinking they don't have the capacity for follow-through. And here again, we underestimate them. A frustrated 18-year-old Harper wants us to know:

"Teenage girls are incredibly deep thinking and deep feeling. But we're socialized to be judged. Society beats out of us our strong sense of self-expression."

In the pages that follow, you're going to see society through a teenage girl's eyes. We're living in a world that's yearning to be transformed, as humanity's pain is everywhere, and our shifts toward healing, justice, and change are slow. Teenage girls struggle in this world.

There have been so many articles in American media in the last three years telling us that "teen girls are not okay," "teenage girls report record levels of sadness," and that there is a "mental health crisis for teen girls" . . . yes, I know, welcome to my book.

I will be sharing some distressing statistics about teenage girls' struggles that might be outdated by the time you read this . . . or not. I encourage you to google the same statistic and see if it's changed over time. I really hope that it has, but if not, that tells us something: *We're still doing the same old thing.*

The struggles of teenage girls offer us so much insight into how we can create a different type of world. If you want a teenage girl to feel confident, whole, and empowered, then this conversation is the way forward.

As 17-year-old Lauryn describes: "I wish adults understood that we have a lot of fire in us because there is so much pushing down on us. We have no choice but to push back."

Personally, I've needed to rediscover the teenage girl inside of me who had so much pushing down on her. There is a lot of discussion in the mental health space these days around healing your inner child, but there hasn't been the same focus on the inner teenager. Adolescence is a completely different developmental stage, and it was the period of my life when familial and societal pressures engulfed me. I've been reconnecting with my inner teenager, with a new sense of love and permission for her voice to be heard.

Healing myself in this way has helped me give the teenage girls in my life what I desperately needed when I was their age. There were triggers inside of me that needed to be disarmed in order to connect more deeply with them. By better understanding my inner teenage girl, I've better understood these girls, and I invite you to have the same reflection because I believe it will help you connect to the teenage girl in your life more deeply. I'll be vulnerably sharing parts of my story to model what that can look like. Like the girls I know, I had absorbed the world's fear.

I've now gained clarity on how much fear we instill in girls, and I've witnessed how it keeps a girl quiet, cultivating the scream that feels trapped inside her. This silencing also creates angst. And a teenage girl's angst is powerful.

As 15-year-old Jade told me, "The angst is coming from things not sitting right in my heart. It's not that I want to create a world with more angst. Teenage girls have this fighting spirit because we can so clearly see what's broken."

*Underestimated* reveals what teenage girls want to tell the world about this brokenness. These girls have the solutions, but we need to empower their voices, not silence them. Teenage girls have a fighting spirit that can be a transformative power for good. They have a vision for a future that fills me with hope. Their powerful voices can motivate us to make more courageous choices. Their dynamic emotions can open up our hearts. Their wisdom can teach us how to be more human.

This book will help us create a world that stops underestimating teenage girls. They are a force that we must connect to—not squash, not dismiss, not judge, not change, not minimize, not control, and not fear. Instead, let's listen to and love them exactly as they are.

## CHAPTER ONE

# FEELINGS

*Only in an open, nonjudgmental space*
*can we acknowledge what we are feeling.*[1]
—Pema Chödrön

**M**adelyn is a deeply sensitive 17-year-old girl with a generally calming presence. However, when she pops onto my computer for our regular Thursday FaceTime, she's clearly frazzled and bothered, her distress spilling out of her like a powerful wave.

I ask her to tell me more about it, and she describes the argument she had with her friends earlier that day. I know the argument all too well myself. Trying to schedule a weekend hangout, coordinating everyone's schedules, trying to make everyone happy, and then it all falls apart, and the hard work is lost and goes unappreciated.

As I listen, I think of so many pieces of advice I could give her. With my extra twenty years of experience trying to make plans with friends—I got this. I know exactly what to do to fix this problem for her. I'll tell her what she did wrong and tell her the solution. That's what she wants, right?

Most people reading this book will already know that trying to tell a teenage girl what to do . . . will not end well. Her eyes will glaze over in darkness as she snaps back a vicious tone that cuts off any sense of connection: "Never mind!" "Stay out of it!" "You don't know what you're talking about!" "You don't understand!"

Every parent still seems to walk right into that trap, but I've learned that this instinct to *advise and fix* comes from an overall misunderstanding of what people, all people, truly need in that moment.

I wait until Madelyn is finished describing her turmoil. And then I say, "Yeah, that sucks."

I had been listening to how she described her feelings throughout the story, remembering the *exact words* that she used. I reflect back to her, "I can understand why you'd feel *frustrated* and *annoyed*. I get why you'd be *upset* about your friends disrespecting your time and effort. Especially when your intentions were to simply create a fun time for everyone. That sucks."

Madelyn's entire face and body relax right in front of me. A wave of emotion wells up in her voice as she responds,

"Thanks for listening. None of my friends understood me, they didn't get where I was coming from."

In front of my eyes, I see what looks like an emotional weight lifting from her shoulders as she sits up a little straighter. Her smile is brighter, her tone is lighter, and the connection between us deepens. She felt seen, heard, understood, and all I had to do was agree that her emotions were valid. It wasn't about me fixing something for her, which is generally our first inclination.

It must be *strongly* noted: this isn't manipulation or fake sincerity. I genuinely put myself in Madelyn's shoes and tried to think about how it would make me feel if I were in that situation. By leaning into empathy, it was easier for me to understand and validate her feelings. I gave her the acknowledgment she needed by reflecting her language and experience. She trusted me to listen. She trusted me to receive her exactly as she is, without me jumping to proclaim the lesson of *her* story.

I've come to learn that this is called *holding space*. Maybe you've never heard this term, or maybe you're rolling your eyes because you have heard it—a lot. Either way, I haven't found a better term to use, and until another emerges, holding space is what I'm calling it.

I wish that this way of validating emotions had come naturally to me, but no, this approach was developed through many painful moments of confronting a girl's defenses and cracking my head on the wall of ice that she quickly produced as if she were Queen Elsa herself. The defense of a teenage girl is whip-fast and resolute. It's not to be messed with. And I've come to love it. I look upon it with reverence, because now I see that she's protecting herself. She's putting up a boundary, granted it can carry a biting tone, but it's a tool in her still-developing toolbox.

Adults, on the other hand, find themselves sharing something vulnerable and then patiently listening to other people's advice, judgment, positive spin, minimization, and moral lessons, all the while flashing a fake smile and shoving their annoyed resentments deep into their soul only to be unearthed during the explosion of a midlife crisis. Perhaps we could nip it all in the bud and say, "I didn't ask for advice on this." However, that feels pretty biting as well, because it feels like no one is used to communicating boundaries.

Boundaries seem messy and uncomfortable, and maybe that's because we have very little practice using them? Teenage girls have taught me some good boundary lessons, but I've also learned that an icy boundary isn't necessary if we simply learn how to hold space for each other's feelings.

In particular, I've learned that communication around holding space is key. No one can read another person's mind. The best way to address that is to phrase everything as a question. When I see that a girl is struggling emotionally, I'll ask her:

"What do you need right now? Do you need me to just listen while you vent?"

The answer is often yes, and so I just let her vent.

If I have problem-solving ideas, I ALWAYS ask if she wants my thoughts before I offer them. Interestingly, after I hold space, the girl usually does ask for my advice, key word being *asks* for my advice. It's actually bizarre that we don't simply shut up and listen more often because it seems that it would be a lot easier and spare a lot more hurt feelings.

This idea of holding space has been a critical lesson that I've learned from teenage girls. *When a person listens without commentary to someone's feelings, it creates a healing space where someone can healthily process emotions, feel understood, and deeply connect to their own humanity.*

I've learned that it is absolutely the best way to offer love and support to not only teenage girls but to *everyone.* So why don't people do it more often?

Well, providing that type of space means I need to be comfortable with feelings. Big feelings, which are also known as . . . feelings. Feelings are often big, but we're so adept at blocking, avoiding, ignoring, and suppressing them that when we see a teenage girl FEELING HER FEELINGS, it can seem like a lot.

Teenage girls are renowned for feeling their feelings. It's pretty much assumed that if you have a daughter, you need to prepare yourself for some type of emotional roller-coaster-obstacle-course-Olympic-race that you've already lost, fallen off the rails, and stumbled into a pile of mud that's now smeared all over your face. Basically, parents of teenage girls are told "Good luck," but you will definitely be destroyed. And the powerful ammunition that those girls yield? Big feelings.

When I asked girls what they wished adults would better understand about them, there were *a lot* of thoughts around expressing their emotions.

Fifteen-year-old Keisha told me: "I wish my parents would just let me express my feelings. If I'm sad, they just don't understand. They make it seem like I'm not tough enough."

Fourteen-year-old Viola shared: "Our hormones aren't what make us emotional and have feelings. Everyone has feelings, we're just feeling them."

Some of the biggest feelings I've encountered with teenage girls have been around college applications. It's particularly more intense when they have the pressure of being the first generation in their family to be applying or don't have access to resources that can assist with the process. Big feelings appear whether it's an application for a community college, an Ivy League school, or while figuring out if college is possible, affordable, or the right next choice. Even for the girls who are incredibly lucky to have a lot of support around applications and financial resources, the process is still treacherously emotional, navigating both extreme internal and external expectations. College seems to reflect a teenager's entire future, dreams, parental dynamic, happiness, potential for success, and self-worth all rolled into one decision of acceptance or rejection. And there is . . . So. Much. Uncertainty.

Uncertainty and a lack of control are profoundly uncomfortable. I would absolutely love to tell a parent that I can unquestionably help their daughter get into her dream college. But I can't. So instead, I swim around in the whirlpool of uncertainty trying to keep everyone—parents and kids—from choking on and drowning in their worries, perceived control, and identity crisis that always seems to occur during the college application process. It's uncomfortable, and I hold a lot of space for a lot of feelings.

When a teenage girl comes to me with sobs and anxiety about college, another choice I have is to avoid and ignore her feelings. I could power through, pushing her toward endless deadlines and perfect essays. I've tried this.

Seventeen-year-old Joon would sit at her dining room table, looking at me in a panic three times a week. Everything in her life seemed to depend on her getting into Yale. And when she sank deep into her anxious feelings, I would steer her back to the tasks at hand without truly listening to her.

In my avoiding and ignoring her feelings, I didn't hear her or understand her needs. I was too uncomfortable and worried about her achieving a very specific outcome, and there were parental pressures as well. She was verbally saying that Yale was her dream school, but then why did discussions of the University of Michigan seem to light her up from within? I can remember our conversations, and looking back, I can now hear her feelings being expressed with brand-new clarity. Her feelings around Michigan were excited, inquisitive, and inspired. Her feelings around Yale were anxious, overwhelmed, scared, and insecure. Instead of spending time with those feelings, acknowledging them, letting her feel them fully, *we powered through.*

"Powering through" is a habit often formed early on in life in order to avoid uncomfortable feelings. It's a coping mechanism that emerges when we are presented with uncertainty. While this tool could end up helping to produce straight As on a report card, at the same time, it also cuts us off from a valuable connection to our emotions. Growing up, I used to think that if there was no solution around an emotion, then why bother allowing myself to feel it? That would be indulgent of me.

Like many girls, this conditioning descended upon me in my teenage years when my feelings were so big that they were scary. It seemed like no one in my life could handle my feelings, so it wasn't safe to express them. That fear and lack of safety led to shutting down and powering through.

Joon and I were caught in that zone of stuck feelings because we were powering through applications too fast to even realize what she was feeling. We couldn't slow down to acknowledge where Joon really hoped to go to college because it would require more courage and vulnerability. Joon and I would also need to have a very difficult conversation with her parents. They were very focused on smaller, New England schools with more prestigious names. I now vividly see how Joon and I wrapped ourselves up in the "go, go, go, do, do, do" intensity of applications that it felt like there wasn't even time to process her feelings that she was excited by the idea of a larger school and not being in New England. It takes time to process feelings, and I've learned the hard way that fear will cut off that flow. We were so cut off that Joon didn't even apply to Michigan.

And Joon didn't get into Yale. She ended up going to Amherst, where she was very unhappy. During her second year, Joon found herself working on her application to transfer. This application process was different—I took so much time to *listen* to not only her words but also her feelings. Starting junior year, Joon would finally find herself at the University of Michigan, where she was profoundly happier. We both reflect on that time as a situation that taught us both necessary and meaningful lessons, but I still wish that I had heard her the first time.

I wish that I had slowed down our process to give enough space for *all* of her authentic feelings.

Today, whether it's about applying to college or having a fight with a friend, I actively invite a teenage girl to join me in that space with the simple question "How do you feel about that?"

I give her time to share, listening with no judgment and a lot of care. If she's struggling to find the words, I don't project one emotion onto her, but instead give her options so she can still find it for herself.

"Are you feeling anxious, frustrated, disappointed, worried? Any feelings are welcome here, even the hard ones." After I listen and reflect her feelings, making sure she knows that I heard and understood them, I will often follow up with one of my favorite questions:

"How can I support you in this?"

This simple question will open surprising doors for connection with not only a teenage girl but with everyone in your life. These types of questions are compiled in the appendix for easy review, and I invite you to use them for countless situations.

When a girl is expressing feelings, her response to this question is often "Just listening helps. No one has acknowledged that this is hard." Teenage girls soften in this space because they're feeling heard and understood.

If she responds to this question with "I don't know," then I recommend just going with it, and keeping it really simple and easy: "Okay, all good. No pressure here."

This type of rapport can take time and it's important to meet her where she's at. A girl might not yet have the words for the type of support she needs, and overall, I find that girls and adult women, myself included, are still learning how to connect with and understand their own needs. I'll explore this more in the chapter People-Pleasing, but there are conversation techniques that can create more space for that discovery.

I find that people, including teenage girls, open up when you meet them exactly where they're at, *with no agenda*. This means having no desired outcome and my tone has no traces of "I want you to agree with me" or "I want you to learn/understand this." I need to be really honest with myself about this because a teenage girl will sniff out motive and judgment with animal instincts that can perceive a threat miles away. And if my honest reflection makes me realize that I do have an agenda, then I need to work to let go of that first.

Trusting myself to really listen, judgment-free, will help these conversations thrive.

As I was writing this book, in spring 2023, AI had just started gaining traction in our daily lives, and the very first reactions from teenage girls were really noteworthy to me. They had started to ask the My AI chatbot on Snapchat for advice on their problems, already calling it their therapist and best friend. That seemed like a quick jump, and I knew there was a reason. I dove in with questions, seeking to understand, and learned that the AI chatbot *doesn't judge them.* That is why they feel connected to it and trust it with their problems.

To create human connection that can offer her nonjudgmental support, *keep communication phrased as a question, with a tone of genuine curiosity.* It gives her a feeling of respect and slows down the process to create more understanding.

This emotional understanding allows the relationship to expand into expressing positive emotions as well. While powering through emotions seems like it's a successful tool to avoid difficulty, it's actually a mechanism that closes us off from our truthful, emotional center. When I shut off my emotions, it also affects my ability to feel uplifting emotions, such as love, appreciation, joy, peace, and hope.

I grew up learning that there are "good" feelings and "bad" feelings, and if I work hard enough and do everything "right," then I won't feel those bad feelings. This is of course not possible, since hardship is part of absolutely every human being's life, but this truth didn't stop me from powering through under the false pretense, clinging to the hope that I could avoid pain. But in that avoidance, I cut off my vulnerability and consequently my authentic connection with others.

I see that feeling of disconnection in teenage girls when there aren't safe spaces for them to express themselves. When people learn that I work with teenage girls, one of the first things they bring up is how girls are "mean." I'll expand on this in the chapter Friends, but unfortunately, I need to unequivocally say to everyone: *Girls are not innately mean.* It's not a set characteristic that we can just conveniently blame. I see girls be mean when they *don't feel emotionally safe.*

This state of fear and disconnection can be very dark. I've witnessed girls descend into isolation because the world is telling them "I'm judging your emotions," which feels the same to her as "You're not accepted for who you are."

Feeling isolated and alone in one's feelings can take quite a toll. For people in the United States ages ten to twenty-four, the suicide rate increased 57.4 percent from 2007 to 2018.[2] Unfortunately, I've had many girls share with me that they've had suicidal thoughts, and I've guided these girls toward therapists and free counseling services, where there has been a lot of progress. Several girls have shared how they've struggled with self-harm through cutting. They were not asking me to help them to stop cutting, which they already had support for, but they were wanting someone to simply listen to their pain with love and care, and absolutely no shame and judgment. Simple responses go a long way:

"That's so hard." "I'm so sorry you're going through this." "Of course you feel upset." "It makes sense you feel that way."

If I jump to positivity, fixing, or powering through, then their emotional wall will go back up, and they probably won't talk to any adult about it. Instead, I acknowledge the struggles that they face as teenagers.

Everyone and everything in a girl's life is telling her what she "should" do or who she "should" be, so of course it can feel unsafe for her to share feelings and her authentic self. Soft-spoken and shy 17-year-old Izzy tensely furrows her brow, as she tries to express her feelings with me about this:

"Everyone is just so scared. My feelings will get so overwhelming that I start wondering if they're valid, because my family can't handle hearing them. So instead of processing them, I resist. I think adults are scared of my big feelings because they're not connected to their own big feelings. It's hard for them to have a moment of empathy and meet you where you're at."

Izzy is wisely sharing this common theme I've observed that when a teenage girl boldly expresses her big feelings, and she's met with a resistant, analytical, or dismissive parent, she learns that her vulnerability and true self aren't welcome there. While the parent thinks they're helping by "solutioning" her problem, it actually has the reverse effect, forcing her to cling even harder to what she knows to be true.

A parent might disagree with her, but it doesn't matter. Their daughter is her own person going through her own experience, one that is completely valid. Her feelings aren't flawed. Her feelings are sometimes the only thing that feels true and honest to her.

Girls are also grappling with a society that not only doesn't make space for their feelings but also chooses to stigmatize them. The stereotypes around a teenage girl's identity as "mean," "emotional," "hormonal," and "crazy" are filled with shame, not respect.

This paradigm needs to be reframed. I like to think of a teenage girl's feelings as a punk rock band with lots of eclectic instruments. Everyone is playing loudly and passionately, boldly breaking musical rules, succumbing to intense rhythms, not sounding agreeably melodic, and discovering the dramatic and the eccentric.

On the other hand, most adults share their feelings like a muffled flute, trying to sound pleasing, but really, we're only hearing a suppressed version of a person.

I'm not saying that we should be reckless and reactive with our feelings. Safely and healthily dealing with feelings will be expanded upon, but first, we must acknowledge that these feelings even exist. Every human has fears, insecurities, disappointments, worries, frustrations, resentments. And as the person on the other end of them, it can feel painfully vulnerable to sit with all of that and hold space for the person who is grappling with these emotions.

Someone listening to your muffled flute isn't going to make you feel better because it's not an honest reflection of what you're feeling. We all need someone nodding their head and jamming out to our full-blown punk beat without trying to stop or improve our song.

In my teenage years, I was too scared to let an adult hear the full glory of my punk rock band, because I believed they wouldn't like the music. As 18-year-old Nora notes, "There is a lot of fear of how our parents will react to our feelings and what we have to say. We have a fear of not being heard, even by our parents."

My parents were incredibly logical and practical, so when it came to feelings, they only had the tools that their parents handed down to them, meaning I come from a long familial line of Productive, Efficient, Powering-Through Champions. I became very talented at overthinking, which made me feel like I was intelligent because the focus was on my brain, not my emotions. However, with such clarity now, I can see this as a defense mechanism that no longer serves me.

I had piled all my punk instruments, often unconsciously, into a tiny closet within myself, since that seemed like the easiest and most pain-free path forward.

That closet has since been wrenched open by the intensity of life, and those old punk instruments have been spilling out. It turns out that my overthinking "intelligence" gave me stress, insomnia, insecurity, control issues, and anxiety. Alternatively, learning from teenage girls' wise emotions has helped me open a new door for my inner teenage girl and release her big feelings.

And what is a safe and healthy space for that release now? I've learned that it's simply identifying the feeling and then feeling it. Harvard-trained neuroscientist Dr. Jill Bolte Taylor has researched how an emotion triggers "a 90 second chemical process that happens in the body; after that, any remaining emotional response is just the person choosing to stay in that emotional loop . . . This means that for 90 seconds you can watch the process happening, you can feel it happening, and then you can watch it go away."[3] Naming the emotion during this process has proven to be an effective part of completing the cycle as well.

Ninety seconds to let an emotion pass through a person versus decades of stuffing the feelings in a closet and powering through. Wow, I wish I had known about that earlier!

That said, I know what it feels like to be scared of acknowledging really painful feelings—maybe the emotions won't end, and I'll get depressed, and I'll be no fun to be around, and I won't be able to find a solution to stop feeling them.

Ironically, I've learned that emotional regulation *is* the solution. The National Institutes of Health identifies some *dysfunctional* emotional regulation strategies as "rumination and emotion suppression."[4] Their research shows that this type of overthinking and suppression of feelings leads to the pathogenesis of depression and physiological disease. To address this issue, their research also demonstrates how feeling the feelings in a safe space (constructive emotional regulation) reduces the potential.

Noticing and naming the specific feelings is at the forefront of emotional regulation techniques, and mindfully creating space and acceptance around that emotion is helpful too. Therapists can offer more options, and I encourage everyone to explore what works for them.

I just want to emphasize that teenage girls have already instinctually known that feeling big feelings is a healthy and normal part of being human before any research supported it. Nora expanded on her thoughts with me: "It's helpful to let feelings happen because you see a lot of different sides of the feelings that you didn't see before when you were holding them in."

Society has been so busy dismissing girls as "dramatic" that we've missed the wisdom they can offer us.

I've worked really hard to incorporate this wisdom into my own life. When I was recently grieving a friend's death, I had a wave of emotion overcome me at a birthday party. In people's discomfort with seeing such emotions in a social setting, they immediately shared platitudes, working toward the goal that I think a lot of us have been taught: *End the tears as fast as possible, by any means necessary.*

Thankfully, a friend pulled me aside and held some space for me to cry, which lasted only a minute or so. I named the feelings of sadness and grief that were happening in the moment, and then the feelings passed. I felt so much better afterward, and it felt so healthy to process the feelings in real time.

By stuffing down those moments in the past, I would feel scared of big feelings because I didn't have the language to express myself. Thankfully, now I'm equipped with a Feelings Wheel next to my desk with 130 different feelings to choose from, because I've needed help to find the words.

I've included the wheel in Appendix 1 because it's a really helpful tool that I've used with teenage girls when they're trying to process their feelings. It starts at the center with basic feelings like "good," "bad," "numb," "sad," "angry," and expands into more specific emotions, providing more nuance and clarity. If a girl tells me she's feeling sad, then I can offer some more expressive options:

"Does the sadness you're feeling have layers to it, like disappointed, lonely, hurt?"

When we land on the right word, she feels more understood. When she can express her feelings more accurately, I often see relief wash over her.

I think of Nora telling me, "When you keep feelings inside, it's a lot harder to move past them. It's important to ask what's the best way to deal with them, work through them, and understand them."

She helped me realize that, like teenage girls, I'm a human being who needs to feel, not just think. And I want to offer her that same gift.

When I hear a teenage girl's punk rock band of feelings, my ears perk up. What if she simply gets to process the feeling *now*, and not decades later, wouldn't that be great?! We all need this type of support, to be able to freely show our emotions and have someone hold space for us around them. Teenage girls have shown me that power. They've helped me connect more deeply with the people around me, revealing that we're all normal human beings who simply have . . . big feelings.

Girls don't exaggerate their feelings. I see people blame a girl's feelings on things like her period, but a girl can have feelings without her period. The actual problem is that people don't try to understand her. —ROSY, AGE 15

---

✦ Judging someone's feelings and trying to fix them with unsolicited advice or positive spin only makes a person put up more walls and feel misunderstood.

✦ People need someone to simply listen, holding space for their difficult feelings, helping them feel heard and understood. Ask the question: "Do you want advice or space to vent?"

✦ Constructive emotional regulation involves feeling and naming emotions in the moment instead of powering through and suppressing them.

✦ BIG feelings are normal. Creating fear and judgment around them won't help in processing them.

✦ Feeling difficult and painful emotions is part of being human, and it's through that vulnerability that we can more deeply connect with one another.

## CHAPTER TWO

# CHOICE

*The more decisions that you are forced to make alone,*
*the more you are aware of your freedom to choose.*[1]
—Thornton Wilder

Holding space for a teenage girl's feelings, without telling her what to do, will eventually lead to a moment where she has to make a choice for herself. She will need to decide if and how she'll respond to whatever is causing her emotional pain. This means that you may have to bear witness to a choice that you wouldn't make yourself, a choice that you worry might cause her pain, or a choice that you might consider to be "wrong." Which. Is. TOUGH. I'm not saying that this lesson has been easy to learn, but wow have I seen some unexpected rewards.

Teenage girls have profoundly taught me how to *invite and respect someone's choice when it comes to making a decision.*

Brianna is a strong-willed 13-year-old with a big heart, but it takes some effort to crack her tough exterior. Her family and teachers were all angry that Brianna couldn't seem to wake up on time to avoid being late for her first-period class at school. School administrators were emailing about what a huge issue it had become, and I could see her grade suffering as a result. Everyone wanted to punish Brianna until her behavior changed. It didn't seem to be working because she's always up for a fight, and she's more likely to dig in her heels when confronted. When I sat down with her to talk about it, I phrased everything as a question. This will come up a lot, but it needs to be emphasized that a "You *should* do this" approach will not be effective. Instead, with a lot of respect I ask, "Brianna, do you want to get good grades in school?"

"Yeah . . ."

"Do you think your tardiness is affecting your grades?"

"Yeah . . ."

"Then why are you waking up late?" Brianna looked at me with both annoyance and respect that my logic flow was leading her down a path she couldn't avoid. I waited patiently with no pressure or frustration in my tone.

Brianna took a deep breath and sighed heavily. "My parents took my phone away and it had my alarm clock on it." I almost laughed out loud at the simplicity of it all, but I knew better, because a teenager's phone is a VERY SERIOUS MATTER. Instead, I held some space.

"Okay, that sucks. I would absolutely hate to have my phone taken away." Brianna nodded with angst and pain washing over her face. I continued: "It's hard to be in an angry place with your parents. Is there any hope of getting the phone back anytime soon?"

"No," she said resolutely and hopelessly. At that point, I could have offered so many solutions. There is probably an obvious one blaring loudly in your mind, but if I say it, I lose hope of the idea being accepted. So instead I continued with questions:

"What's another way you could wake up on time then?"

"I don't know, my mom could wake me up."

"Has that worked in the past? Do you like when she does that?"

"No, I hate it."

"Okay, what's another idea?"

"I don't know," she says, hunching over and letting her head fall onto the desk, trying to show me that she's given up. That's always a sign that it's time for me to get super real and humorously sarcastic. I'm a big fan of using sarcasm with teenagers. Not with a condescending tone, definitely not, but rather using a playful, exaggerated tone that calls out the truth.

"Really? Huh. Is there nothing in the entire world that could wake someone up other than a cell phone? There aren't any devices that have been invented? Wow, that sucks . . . maybe you should invent something like that? I mean, it could make millions of dollars!"

Brianna looks up with her sly eyes and cracks a smile. We sit there in silence for a bit. I've become comfortable in that zone where there's no guarantee that a teenage girl will make a good choice for herself. With levity, I ask,

"So how would you like to handle this? Whatever you want is fine with me." I say this using a severe amount of chill and mindfulness in order to legitimately achieve a nonjudgmental tone.

Brianna knows I'm telling the truth because I've put the choice in her hands so many times before that I've built trust. She knows that this decision is fully *hers*.

"I could get an alarm clock," she manages to utter.

"Oh really? What's that? That sounds cool."

Brianna laughs at my lighthearted sarcasm. "I just hate alarm clocks with lots of buttons. They confuse me."

"Yeah, I get that, I've been confused too. How about we pull up some options on the computer, and we can find exactly the type of buttons you want. You pick it out."

She smiles and says, "Okay, fiiine."

To this day, every morning, Brianna uses the alarm clock that she picked out. She stopped being late for school and her grade in her first-period class improved. Brianna's mother exclaimed to me, "She's had alarm clocks before, and this is the only one that's ever worked for her! I can't believe it, you figured Brianna out, you're the Teenage Girl Whisperer!"

Oof. That label . . . is so *wrong*. A "whisperer" quiets and silences something that is seemingly too out-of-control. Let's be clear, a teenage girl is not a horse that needs to be subdued. In this moment, I did the opposite of quieting. I allowed Brianna to have her own voice. By giving her a choice, I put the control in her hands.

This example provides a relatively easy solution of an alarm clock, but I've learned that this style of questioning and letting a girl have the choice in the solution can translate to almost every problem she faces. I've found that not only does this approach increase accountability and ownership of her choices, but it also motivates her to make the solution work, because it's *her* solution. She wants her solution to be successful, therefore she'll be more invested and engaged right from the start.

There are a couple of phrases I lean on pretty heavily when I'm in difficult conversations with girls. The best starting point is usually "What are your thoughts on _____?"

It's a question that engages her mind, respects her thoughts, and involves her in the process. I keep a lighthearted tone and overall ease that has no agenda. I always *invite her consent*, even in small details such as, "Do you want me to send you a reminder text about that?"

By inviting her choice, she can't shove me into the "You're trying to control me" box. With my respectful tone, she also can feel that I genuinely care about her answer to the question "How would you like to handle it?"

If I disagree with her opinion, I usually say,

"Huh. That's interesting, I hadn't thought of it like that. What are your thoughts on . . . ?" and I bring up another aspect, and we discuss. The conversation doesn't shut down because I stay in a state of genuine curiosity, so that I can't be mistaken for telling her what to do. Additionally, I always try to enthusiastically agree with her whenever I can. Agreement, actively spoken out loud, helps her feel understood.

Fourteen-year-old Viola, while still struggling to find herself in middle school, impressed me with her wisdom when she told me what she wants adults to know about teenage girls:

"We know what we're doing. We know what the 'right' decision is, but we may still choose to make decisions that aren't the smartest option. We want to have that freedom."

A fact that has infuriated and exasperated parents for all of eternity.

Watching a kid or anyone you love make the wrong decision and then suffer consequences for that mistake is soul-crushingly difficult.

However, I've learned from a teenage girl that when it was *her* choice in the first place, then it's also *her* mistake to own and learn from. And if it's *hers* to own, then she learns from it so much more thoroughly and quickly. If the choice is forced upon her, then the learning process is polluted by blame, landing in the classic realm of "You made me do it."

I used to spend a lot of time protecting teenage girls from bad choices, but it often felt like I was just delaying the inevitable. I would offer guidance if she asked for it, but unfortunately, history continues to prove that pain is still life's greatest teacher. Basically, I found that my interference of buffering her consequences often ended up blocking the learning process.

That said, it has still been incredibly difficult to release my hopes for a specific outcome. I heard an acronym that's popular in the 12-step recovery world that has helped me find more space in my heart to allow for this release—it's really a release of *perceived* control—letting go of the illusion that I can control this teenage girl (or anyone for that matter) and convince her to make the "right" decision. The acronym is L.O.V.E., which stands for Let Others Voluntarily Evolve. I now consider it an act of LOVE to let people simply make their own decisions about their life.

People will grow and learn on their own time, and I've found that the more I try to force that growth, the more it backfires. Yes, teenage girls are still young, and we have the urge to protect them, but I see that protection backfire more often than I see it succeed. When we question her choices, she's more likely to stubbornly swear an oath of loyalty to that bad choice just to spite us.

Listening to her questionable choice, holding space for her differing opinions and feelings, and responding with no judgment or advice (unless she asks for it), is a special type of psychological jujitsu that can have surprising rewards.

The best example that I have of this jujitsu in action is a story from my own years as a teenage girl. I was the type of teenager who was always "over" high school and who had been ready to be an adult by the age of twelve. At seventeen, I thought high school boys were dumb and boring, so when I connected with a twenty-year-old deep-thinking, soulful college guy with a sweet smile, I was delighted. Our three-year age difference could be considered controversial and even illegal if we were sexually active. I was turning eighteen soon, but perhaps even more controversial was the fact that he was a summer volunteer with the youth group at my church. We connected after he left his volunteer role, but looking back on this choice, I now see myself as a total renegade.

Most teenage girls would hide this from their dad out of fear. Not me. I thought it was a respectful and responsible choice to tell him. How did I arrive at that type of thinking? We'll get to that. But first, there I am . . . sitting with my dad in the car, driving home from dinner, and with a calm voice, I say, "Dad, I want you to know I've started dating Max Stevens. You met him that one time at church." I stare at him, hunting for a reaction, but my dad keeps driving with not even a glimmer of turmoil on his face.

We can all imagine the classic, stereotypical reactions we've come to expect from dads who feel it's necessary to protect their "little girl." At this point, many dads would pummel their daughter with questions: "How old is he?" "Is that appropriate?" "How long has this been going on?"

Or many dads would get angry and try to control the situation: "No way!" "He's too old for you!" "He can't be trusted!" "You will never see him again!"

Many dads would worry about what other people might think—friends, church people, family—there's never a lack of judgment surrounding our choices on any given day. Instead, with a calm and loving tone, my dad said, "Thanks for telling me, Chelsey. If you've chosen to date him, then he must be a really great guy. I trust that you would only choose an incredible guy who treats you really well. I'm glad you told me, thank you."

My eyes widen as I hold back a gasp. My brain is immediately flooded with forceful thoughts: *Wait . . . is Max good enough?!? My dad trusts me to make this decision. Have I chosen an incredible enough guy for me?? My dad respects my choices, so have I made the right choice, because I deserve a guy who will treat me really well!?*

In that one single moment, my dad flipped on a light bulb inside me that remains lit to this day. The glowing light of Self-Trust and Self-Respect has illuminated all of my romantic decisions. I have always chosen really high-quality guys in my life. And when my husband, Charles, attempted to ask for my dad's blessing to propose, it was no surprise that my dad responded:

"Ask HER."

I don't think Charles should have asked my dad at all, because it reflects a sexist tradition that originates from the idea that my father owns me until he gives permission to another man to take ownership. But unfortunately, our societal narratives and pressures around masculinity seem to be evolving at a much slower rate. A lot of you might have been reading about my teenage romance and thinking, "Sure, I trust the girl, but I don't trust the guy!"

We definitely need to ignite a much longer discussion about the large amount of time and energy we need to invest in supporting young boys with expansive conversations. In the meantime, we could also teach young women to trust themselves to make their own good decisions.

If my dad had responded with any of those earlier, angry versions of questioning, doubting, and controlling, how would I have responded?

I would have furiously continued the relationship in secret. I would have started lying to my dad and feeling shame about the entire situation. A shame like that, involving love and sexuality, would have likely pushed me toward bad life choices and stuck around for decades.

Both of my parents ended up adoring Max, and the relationship was not just some dumb fling to be rebellious and get attention. A lot of adults like to dismiss teenage girls' choices as such. My dad trusted that I would discover exactly what this romance was, on my own, and I did. Which is why I told my dad about it in the first place. Starting from a very young age, my parents always gave me a large amount of trust. I would have that trust until I broke it, which was a very empowering experience for me.

I've found that teenage girls crave trust. But unfortunately, instead, I see parents instill a lot of fear in them.

Now 20 years old, Tara shared how it still affects her: "My parents have always led with fear, which has made me struggle as an adult. Being exposed to more choices in college, I've had no sense of moderation or self-regulation, making worse mistakes than I've needed to, because I wasn't given a chance to learn or feel trust. Fear is not a teacher."

Fourteen-year-old Juliette told me, "My parents think they're protecting me, but I need to make mistakes. I'm not going to learn if they only teach me to be scared. It doesn't work like that."

I think that I'm particularly passionate about this topic because I'm a person who has really benefited from having parents who weren't fearful of me making mistakes.

When I was 13 I went on a road trip with my dad and my 17-year-old brother. My brother drove while I juggled several map books to navigate our way there, during the Wild West time before smartphones and Google Maps existed. Somewhere deep into Arizona, I navigated a wrong turn. We were lost. My dad sat in the back seat and repeatedly and lovingly said, "You'll figure it out."

As my brother and I struggled, our trip got longer and longer. I grappled with feelings of self-doubt and wanting to give up. But after two hours, I finally found our way back to the correct road. In that moment, a new trust in myself blossomed, knowing that if I ever got lost, *I could figure it out*.

I'm guessing that my dad didn't want to be in the car for an extra two hours, but it was way more important to him not to step in and solve my problem for me. It was *my* mistake to fix, and his trust in me, not fear, only helped me get to the solution faster. The same way that my dad's trust in my romantic decision inspired me to evaluate the choice even more. I was asking myself, *Is Max good enough for me?* My dad didn't need to ask, because he was *teaching and trusting me to do it for myself.*

Teenage girls have taught me how to have these same empowering conversations. The art of allowing room for *choice* can be found in every topic of this book. A girl will tell me about her gossiping friends, and I'll say, "How do you wanna handle it?"

Or she'll ask me if she should argue a test grade with a teacher, and I'll say, "What do you think?"

Or her grades might start dropping, and I'll ask, "What do you think the first step is?"

Or my overall favorite . . . "What do you think the solution is?"

Of course, there will come a day when a teenage girl is doing something that a parent truly has a rule about. It could be what she's wearing, what she's posting on social media, or who she's hanging out with. Conversations around these topics will be explored and modeled in further depth throughout the book, but the best overall idea I can offer is: *Seek to understand her first.*

Implementing a hard-line rule in the name of "protecting" a girl often feels faster and easier. I get it. But that said, parents can't offer protection if a girl doesn't feel safe enough to talk in the first place.

When an adult starts a conversation with a teenage girl with genuine curiosity, not hunting for a specific response or behavior change, something deeper happens. She ends up learning the tools to protect herself. Maintaining that same nonjudgmental tone, the conversation could start as simply as "I want to hear your perspective on this. I want to understand better. So can I ask you more questions about it?" If she has a reluctant response, I would follow up by framing the conversation with more safety and clear intentions:

"I have no agenda with these questions. My intention is to better understand your perspective. There's no right or wrong answer." However, it's important to only say these things if they're true for you. If she says, "You just want to get me to agree with you," try to be as honest as possible. I'll expand more on this in the chapter Radical Honesty, but teenage girls will respect the absolute truth. You can respond with:

"Maybe. It's hard to get out of that pattern. But I'm also trying to let go of an outcome because I genuinely want to hear you out. I'm trying to get better at listening." If she ends up sharing more with you, don't turn it into a debate. I would give her time to feel heard with:

"Okay, that's interesting, let me think about that more."

If a teenage girl feels heard and understood, she might actually change her choice to align with her parents. Or she could begrudgingly follow the rule, but she will be happy (even if she doesn't show it) that at least her voice was respected in the conversation. Parents might also change their minds after better understanding her perspective and feelings. Either way, asking the right questions to help her deeply consider her choices is the path to empowerment.

I've now continued this practice of inviting someone's perspective and choice with everyone in my life, and as a result, so much trust and respect has been developed in my relationships. When my husband kept complaining about going to the doctor, I stopped making his appointments (which I hated doing anyway). When a really painful health issue arose, I gave him a hug and let him know that I loved him and that I knew he would figure it out. I was definitely worried about his health, and I wanted to protect him by helping, but these weren't my choices to make. He was befuddled at first, stalled, complained, but after two weeks of a lot of pain, he found himself a doctor. A doctor that he LOVES. No one is more surprised than me at how often he visits this doctor. But this doctor was *his choice*.

I didn't know how much I was inserting myself into other people's decisions until I started taking this different approach. As adulthood beat me up, I developed habits of thinking more control would make me feel secure. I know clearly now that I don't want anyone messing with my choices, so why would I mess with someone else's?

When I witness a teenage girl who isn't allowed to make her own choices, I see doors close inside her. But you don't have to believe me on this, just ask the girls in your life what they think.

Grappling with her patterns of trying to make everyone around her happy, 16-year-old Shanaya vigorously told me, "We need room to have a voice. We're held to an impossible standard, but it's okay to mess up. Boys are allowed to be messy! But the truth is, if I can't make my own choices, then what's the point? Then I'm not really living for myself. I'm living for other people and society."

Seventeen-year-old Izzy feels like her parents control a lot of her decisions, and she painfully struggled to tell me, "When I don't have choices, I feel trapped and shackled down to live in a world I don't want to live in. If no one is listening to me, and I'm not making my own choices, I'm terrified. Because then I have to follow their guideline, and I'm scared that if I break it, then I'll be held down more. Adults think they're doing what's best for me, but instead I just feel caged."

Caged. Trapped. Shackled. Living for other people . . .

Is this what we want for teenage girls?

This is why they want to scream! Why are we still living in a world where girls feel like this?

I don't want anyone on this planet to feel caged or trapped.

Teenage girls are reflecting a much larger conversation that we all need to have. Choice reflects a human being's autonomy and therefore their ability to pursue their own happiness. I've found that squashing a girl's choices closes her off to not only the people who love her, but to herself as well. Alternatively, if she's encouraged to step through those closed doors, she can experience trust, self-respect, growth, and an authentic path toward her own happiness.

I see the people around teenage girls, out of fear slam those doors shut, scared she will make the "wrong" choice. But she's not even being given the chance to make the "right" choice.

*We are underestimating her.*

Some people argue that she's young and dumb, but what if she's not? What if she has her own internal wisdom that hasn't been given a voice? What if she simply needs someone to trust her and believe in her?

My parents have trusted me with a lot of choices, which has helped me to become a more present person to my life, choosing my own schedule and activities that make me happy.

Having this sense of agency also makes my relationship with my parents so much better. —MIRA, AGE 16

---

✦ Inviting and respecting teenage girls' consent and choice in decisions motivates them to take ownership over the solutions and make them work.

✦ People learn from their mistakes more thoroughly and quickly if it was their choice in the first place, otherwise blame will pollute the potential for learning.

✦ Interfering or buffering someone's consequences ends up blocking the learning process.

✦ Before protecting or controlling, seek to understand first, with curiosity, not judgment.

✦ Not being able to make your own choices shuts you off from your authentic sense of self and agency in the world.

## CHAPTER THREE

# SEXUALITY

*There is no way to repress pleasure*
*and expect liberation, satisfaction, or joy.*[1]
—adrienne maree brown

've found that the topic of a teenage girl's sexuality exposes the most gripping, overpowering, alarming, toxic, and understandable fears. It's a space full of so many charged opinions that I'm certainly going to step in some shit here. But I'm up for it. You may disagree with me at times, but having this conversation is too important and cannot be avoided.

This chapter is going to be longer than others because the whole book could be an expansion of this topic. There is so much to learn about a teenage girl's wisdom and power during conversations about sexuality. I'm often the only adult in their life who they feel that they can talk to about sex, and they really want to talk about it. It can be something as minor as "Can I get an STD from kissing?" or as serious as "I might be pregnant, what the fuck do I do?" There have been so many questions about birth control, and so many devastating tears when a girl tells me that she's been sexually harassed or assaulted. I embrace these conversations, connect with parents when needed, and hold space for a whole lot of feelings.

As often as I witness words like *pregnant*, *STIs*, or *rape* ignite people's fear of a teenage girl's sexuality, I also see the words *pleasure*, *orgasm*, and *clitoris* ignite just as much fear, possibly more. This conversation is all just one big forest fire ignited by fear. So, let's do this . . . let's jump into the fire together, feel the heat, maybe even get burned, but still, hopefully, learn how we can eventually turn this into a campfire where everyone is sitting around discussing, laughing, learning, and having a good time.

With teenage girls, the conversation around sex usually starts with a question like "No one wants to talk with me about sex, in a real way. Is there a class at school that's going to cover it in more depth?"

Hmmm, well, according to the Guttmacher Institute, as of 2023, only 25 states require that public schools teach both sex and HIV education, *with only 17 of them requiring that the information be "medically accurate."* Meanwhile, 29 states require an emphasis on abstinence.[2]

So . . . with deep anguish over the American sex education debacle, I respond to that wide-eyed, hopeful, curious girl with, "No. It's very unlikely they're going to go into more depth at school."

No one should be assuming that schools have it handled, and parents obviously need to be a focal point for sex education conversations. I've found that a lot of parents are daunted by the task, so I'm working to offer support here. I've had success with girls really opening up to me and sharing their questions and concerns, so I'll be giving tips on how to approach these conversations, with inside info on how teenage girls are thinking about sex and how we can support them.

Overall, I've found that we could all be more courageous in these conversations. A teenage girl's sexuality is the epicenter of society's top-notch squashing, controlling, silencing, dismissing, minimizing, and fearing, and if we continue doing the same thing, the situation will never get better. I've found that adults who didn't get an early education in the topic have had to unpack and heal decades of shame and heavy baggage around sex and sexuality.

When people ask me if I can give explicit advice on "how to talk to your daughter about sex," I often respond:

"Why is it hard for you to talk about it with her? Why do you feel uncomfortable?"

I really recommend examining those answers first. There will be questions throughout this chapter that can help prompt that exploration. A teenage girl will definitely pick up on whatever discomfort or wounds you might still have around sex, and I'm hoping you don't want her to absorb and play out those same wounds. Our wounds are understandable because we've been functioning from a broken system that can't seem to figure out if it's selling sex or afraid of it. However, within my heartfelt conversations with teenage girls, I've learned a poignant lesson: *Rather than working to prevent and judge teenage girls' sexual choices, let's work to create a world that thoroughly educates everyone on sexual responsibility and pleasure.*

I'm going to start by diving into a tough topic because it's the number one thing girls bring up with me. Sexual violence, harassment, and gender double standards. Girls may be hesitant to talk to their parents about sex, but I find that they will talk intellectually about these topics. I *don't* mean a *debate* or a conversation provoking fear about these issues. I mean that teenage girls like to know that their parents are examining these issues with an attitude of "Wow, this is so awful and unfair that girls have to deal with this."

It's a really helpful gateway into building trust and rapport because a girl needs to know that *you're on her team.* A teenage girl can handle these heavier conversations, and for her, it feels extremely frustrating that people aren't talking about America's sexual violence epidemic with more outrage. Without feeling like people are on her team, these issues can block a teenage girl from connecting to a healthy expression of her sexuality.

Every single teenage girl I know who has a large chest has told me at some point that "men are creepy." Seventeen-year-old Riley describes the stares she has to endure when she goes to the gas station, coffee shop, grocery store, or anywhere, really. With a defeated spirit, she's begged me, "I really want the catcalls to stop, or how they undress me with their eyes! Ughhhh, please make it stop!"

Instead of asking Riley how she would like to be supported in this, her parents have endless commentary on Riley's clothes. They believe that if her cleavage finds the light, the shine will be too bright for the men who walk the streets of this world. And for some reason, men lacking sex education who have been socialized to think that it's okay to flagrantly stare at a girl's chest without understanding the impact, are still getting to control the story and dictate Riley's choices.

The social constructs of toxic masculinity that are geared toward violence, fear of emotion, dominance, anger, and entitlement have created a lot of pain around this topic. Under our current system, in 2023 the CDC reported that 14 percent of American teenage girls have been raped at some point in their lives and 18 percent had experienced sexual violence in the previous year.[3] That's really hard to reckon with, and I don't think anyone is okay with these horrific statistics.

I've had so many amazing, supportive men in my life stand by me in addressing these issues, because like me, they agree that a healthy expression of masculinity is in desperate need of exploration and expansion. I'm asking us to consider: Is the rampant sexual assault, objectification, and harassment that comes with men acting "creepy" a product of our collective socialization, lack of sex education, and the undeveloped masculine energy that simply can't hold the powerful container of a teenage girl's sexuality? One thing I know for sure:

*None of this is her fault.*

All of the fear that is directed at her should be directed at addressing the core issues that create male violence. But instead of naming the social problem "violence perpetrated by men," we call it "violence against women." This emphasizes the victim and frames it as a woman's issue, which is so frustrating, because if she had the power, she would have ended the violence by now.

After hearing so many assault stories, I've tried to support girls in this struggle however I can. Alongside inspiring men, I've facilitated conversations within the entertainment industry on how masculinity is portrayed in film and TV and organized events for the nonprofit A Call to Men,[4] which is a violence prevention organization that educates boys and men and promotes healthy manhood. There are men doing exciting work in this space, and I've witnessed how it can help create a world that feels safer for a teenage girl to explore her sexuality.

However, unfortunately, the status quo is still applying a Band-Aid to the problem rather than figuring out what's causing the wound in the first place. I know so many girls learning self-defense in schools across the country, while as of 2023, only 11 states require that boys learn consent within the sex education curriculum . . . 11 states?! Obviously, my inner teenage girl is enraged about all of this, and so are all the girls I talk to. I could have filled this entire book with girls' quotes sharing their agony and fury about sex as it relates to our patriarchal culture. They know the timeless, tragic tale, but again, no one is listening to them.

Seventeen-year-old Hazel read an early draft of this chapter, and at this very point, she wanted to make sure we were all listening when she said, "Girls are taught over and over how not to get raped, but boys aren't explicitly taught to *not rape*. Or not to harass or not to be creepy. It seems like no one is focused on teaching boys how to be better, so that girls can be safe. Go talk to your boys!"

With these conversations in particular, so many girls have told me how frustrated they are with their father, who they wish was more outspoken in his support and showed the same type of outrage about sexual violence that he has for high taxes. Of course, not all fathers are like this, but unfortunately so many girls have brought it up with me that I don't feel comfortable moving forward without noting it. When a father is silent on these issues, he's missing an opportunity to model for his daughter the type of treatment she deserves. If a father is looking for a way in, one example could be to use current events, casually saying to her:

"I was reading about the Harvey Weinstein trial, and it's absolutely horrific that women have to deal with stuff like this. I can't believe 87 women had to come forward in order to make the system hold him accountable. One woman is horrible enough. What are your thoughts on it?" As I've noted before, I recommend listening, agreeing, and showing up for her in the way that she needs. She will most likely be very impressed and touched that you care.

This is one pathway into a conversation that is particularly helpful for fathers, but I have worked with many moms who have desperately asked me how to have more explicit sex-ed conversations with their daughters who immediately shut down when their moms bring up anything. I recently asked a mom to really unleash her questions and fears on me, so I could better understand how to help.

"I just want to know what's going on. Is she having protected sex? Are friends pressuring her to have sex? Are boys pressuring her? Or does she feel ready, and if she does, how can I know if she feels physically, mentally, emotionally safe to do it? I'm scared because it means she's growing up, she's leaving me, she's becoming a woman, she's not my little girl, and I can't protect her anymore. I mean, what if she likes it too much and stops focusing on school because she likes it so much? What if she gets pregnant and it ruins her life? I'm just scared and don't know where to even start."

I'm going to do my best to unpack some of this, but again, the answers could be an entire book, and I direct you to Peggy Orenstein's *Girls & Sex: Navigating the Complicated New Landscape*[5] for a deeper dive. It can be hard to give resources and concrete advice because this cultural conversation is evolving, and it might go in directions I don't expect.

At this moment, I want to lean into the ways we can further conversations and listen to the type of support girls are asking for from parents.

Sixteen-year-old Zandy requested, "Please tell parents to bring up sex with more ease. I feel like they're subconsciously looking at it like their girl is about to *lose* something. It's not a loss of her purity or childhood, that's insane and some bullshit. Don't frame it like a *loss*."

Seventeen-year-old Lauryn told me, "I wish parents wouldn't romanticize it. We know it's a hard topic, and there are stigmas, so let's be real and not sugarcoat it."

Sixteen-year-old Peeta emphasized to me, "Tell parents that how they talk about their own body and sexuality is going to affect our behavior. Oh and tell them that shaming us is really not helpful. It makes us depressed and hate ourselves."

Fifteen-year-old Olivia said, "Just don't come at the conversation with an attitude of 'It's bad if you do this.' I need to feel like a parent is a safe place to go to. I'll open up more if it seems like you're actually going to help rather than judge."

From that mom's whirlwind of questions that she asked me, I know the best source for her answers is her own daughter. But if we don't know where to start, then the harder topics will never be discussed.

I've had a lot of success with some basic starting points into sex-ed conversations, and I'll model an example here. Most importantly, DON'T try to turn these conversations into some covert agenda to gather data on her sex life. That will backfire, horribly. This is about building trust and respect. So, with a tone of ease that is intellectually curious—not a tone that conveys fear or judgment—a parent could start off by saying to her daughter, "I just found out that only eleven states teach boys consent as part of the school's sex education curriculum. Did you know that? That's so horrible." The girl might not know that, and you two can bond over your shared incredulity. She could also respond:

"Yeah, it's so dumb." Then the parent, keeping a super-chill tone that respects the girl's intellect, could ask, "How do you think sex education in schools could be better?" Then listen and agree with her.

With any follow-up, keep it phrased as a question. I like to use consent as an entry point because you might also get lucky and hear more about the topics she wants to learn about. If she shares those, please don't try to teach her your opinions right away. First, explore her thoughts, and then maybe ask, "Do you want to hear my thoughts on that?" Or stay chill and wait for the next time, as this is a process.

A simpler exchange might happen too, with a girl saying: "They could teach us more, instead of only how to deal with our period."

"That's all they're teaching? Wow, yeah, agreed. That's dumb."

Pause and see if she has more to say, but if the energy feels positive and relaxed, sometimes there's also room to empower her own solutions: "Is there anything you'd want to do about it? You'd be so good at talking to the teachers about improving the curriculum."

If she says no, it's not a big deal. I promise she still heard you. She heard you agreeing with her and believing in her. She heard that you're on her team. In general, with exchanges like this, listening, agreeing, and asking questions out of your own curiosity about her intellect are absolutely key. Another good entry-point question is:

"Do you think the media influences a woman's sexuality? Like TV and movies, what do you think they're telling the world about sexuality?"

The media can be a really great portal into these conversations. I'll elaborate more in the chapter The Media, but watching the same TV show is a fantastic, casual way to bring up sexuality topics. Also, I find that instead of *sex*, the word *sexuality* is often easier for girls to engage in because it feels intellectual. Don't be surprised if they veer into LGBTQ+ conversations, which is great, and I'll cover ways to respond later in the chapter Identity.

One thing that's incredibly important as you head into these conversations is to educate yourself on topics that girls might feel shame around, like masturbation, not knowing their anatomy, porn, performative sex, birth control, and STIs. If it feels uncomfortable to talk about these topics, I recommend reading Dr. Emily Morse's *Smart Sex* [6] to examine your own thoughts, education, and experience. There are so many harmful ramifications when a society is not educating its population on sexual health, so we need to prepare ourselves mentally and emotionally.

If you ever get a response from a girl that feels like a block, rather than an answer, such as "I don't know, Mom, it's hard to talk about," just hold space and agree:

"Yeah, agreed. It's hard to talk about." And that's all. I would *not* recommend adding, "But I'm here for you if you want to talk" type of stuff. Whether you mean to or not, a teenage girl will often interpret extra platitudes as a secret intention to get info on her sex life. I'd just go with her flow, keep it simple, and most of all, judgment-free. Meet her where she's at and help her feel understood. That's it!

Of course, these conversations can grow exponentially from here, but it takes time to build trust and rapport. Try telling your daughter that you trust her and see what happens. Trust is a breeding ground that generates more trust, in contrast to the friction and defensiveness of suspicion. By trusting her, you're helping her learn how to trust herself. I've found that teenage girls know a lot more about these issues than you might think, and are often way more responsible than you might think.

One thing teenage girls know for sure is that whatever the situation, their clothes will be blamed. Lauryn told me that if her teenage angst could burn any system down to the ground, it would be dress codes.

I have an endless number of stories from girls who were told their outfit at school was not "appropriate," and were forced to wear a jacket to "cover up" on a sweltering-hot day. I'm continually shocked to learn that, yet again, it was a tank top that showed a bra strap. That's it! Is everyone really that scared of bra straps? When the girl describes the experience to me, it's clear that this fear is creating *so much shame.*

Policing a girl's clothes makes them feel like shit. It tells her that it's *her* problem to manage a boy's sexual urges when obviously it's *his* responsibility. It tells her that a boy's needs are more important than hers. It tells her that her sexuality and body are bad. It tells her that her self-expression through her clothes (something wildly important to a teenager) is dangerous. And it squashes her, big time. Her natural expression of identity is pulverized into little shame-filled bits and pieces.

Instead of teaching boys how to healthily and respectfully process their own sexuality and humanize girls beyond sex objects, we trample teenage girls' choices.

My inner teenage girl has personally felt the ramifications into adulthood. I didn't ask for a large chest when I hit puberty, but wow have I walked through fire for it. When I was getting feedback on publicity photos for my author website, I had a lot of people comment on my cleavage, asking the hard-hitting question: "Should you be showing cleavage if you're discussing teenage girls?" I was told that it would alienate parents if I was being sexy. Is that the only thing my cleavage can communicate? I've always felt like I've had to tough it out and tolerate comments about my cleavage because that's the way the system works. But maybe the system is really hurtful and we can work to change it?

I'm hoping we can all first bring awareness to how these lacerations of shame can leave scars for life. It's taken me years of self-work to find a healing and positive relationship with my body, which has helped me find peace in wearing clothes that might show my controversial cleavage.

In addition to the adults trying to control a teenage girl's self-expression, she also has to contend with toxic media representations that ceaselessly sexualize her value. The pressure to be pretty is like an eight-hundred-pound gorilla ferociously following her everywhere she goes.

Is that why teenage girls love to post sexy photos on their social media feeds? Are they just victims of a toxic culture bent on sexualizing them? That's what I thought, but after talking at length about this with girls, I've learned there is a lot more going on. Does the media have an impact? Of course, and I'll expand on that in later chapters, but there's also a precise generational shift in feminism that I've seen affect this issue.

I grew up during a wave of feminism that was trying to fiercely expand a woman's value beyond her looks and sexuality. I worked tremendously hard to amplify my intelligence, sense of humor, and kindness toward others. It got so intense that I would self-righteously disdain pretty and sexy girls with unwarranted judgment, saying, "They have nothing else going for them."

I'm really embarrassed to admit that, but I can have compassion for my own limiting socialization. I was the type of feminist who played sports, was good in math, bad at cooking, and considered myself a future leader. And I tried not to look too pretty while doing any of that. I hid my voluptuous body under baggy clothes so that I'd be taken seriously and put all my focus on being the smartest person in the room.

So, when the Instagram account of Sophia, a 17-year-old with a charismatic spirit, exploded, and she started to become a "beauty influencer," many of my judgments flared up. I remember one time helping Sophia study for an AP U.S. History test when her mom suddenly stormed through the door. She shoved her phone in Sophia's face and exclaimed,

"You posted this photo? That's way too much skin. Do you know who looks at these photos?!"

I looked at the photo and saw Sophia showing off her pouty lips and her provocative cleavage, looking like a 24-year-old supermodel on a Sunset Strip billboard selling something sexy with her sensual beauty. At least that's what her mom and I think. Sophia looks at her mom with a calm, resolute stare.

"I look good," she says. I meet eyes with Sophia's mom. It's clear she's about to blow. Without Sophia seeing, I mouth to her mom, "I got this."

Her mom takes a deep breath and says, "Talk to Chelsey about it." She flees, trying to escape before the dam breaks on her true thoughts and feelings on the matter. We can't escape the fact that having another trusted adult voice in a girl's life, other than her parents, can be really helpful.

I take a beat and very consciously swallow my knee-jerk judgment. I turn to Sophia and say, "You look really pretty in this photo."

"Yeah? Thank you."

I shift gears to my curious, super-chill question mode that seeks to better understand the intellect of the human being in front of me.

"Does this photo make you feel pretty? Are you hoping for lots of 'likes' on it?"

She rolls her eyes. "It's not about that."

"Okay, cool. Do *you* think you're showing too much skin?"

"I like my skin. I like myself in this photo. It makes me feel like who I want to be."

I nod, hearing her thoughtful, sincere tone. I'm struck by how rare it is for a woman to say, "I like myself." Sophia should like herself; she's an extraordinary teenager. She's academic, generous, ambitious, witty, empathetic, hardworking, organized, athletic. She has way more going for her than her looks. So I ask:

"But aren't you way more than your beauty? Do you feel like being sexy minimizes all the other great parts of who you are?"

"Sexy is one part of who I am. Chelsey, I can be all things. Women can be sexy *and* smart. Isn't that what you taught me about feminism? Women can do and be all things. In this photo, I wanted to explore the sexy part of myself. Is there something wrong with that?"

Oof. Wow. I take a deep breath because I'm clearly in the deep end of the pool.

"Nope. You're right." We share a smile of feminist positivity, but then I take another deep breath because I also never waver from jumping off the diving board to make the biggest splash. Having known Sophia since she was eight, I'd had a *lot* of mature conversations with her by this point, and I was not going to underestimate what she was capable of discussing. So, I leapt into the deep end.

"Are you worried at all that strange men are going to look at this photo and jerk off to you?"

Sophia laughs a little bit, not out of immaturity, but just out of the surprise that someone is willing to be so radically honest with her.

"That's not my problem. I do this for me. My choices shouldn't be dictated by some creepy dude on the internet."

My jaw drops, and I almost give her a standing ovation as my heart explodes with love for this brilliant young woman. Sophia is striving for a world where no one steals her story.

Ideally, it would be a world where everyone is thoroughly educated on sexual responsibility, so like Sophia, we can all feel free to explore all the parts of who we are.

But we're not there yet, are we? Sophia and I continued the conversation with her mom, who really sought to understand Sophia's perspective. We talked through how if she's going to present herself as a sexual being in an adult world, then she still needs to be prepared to get sexual attention. We asked her what type of support she needs around that, and she said, "Just don't make it seem like everything is my fault. Society congratulates boys for sexual conquests, and then tells me I'm bad, like I'm a seductress. Maybe it's not always about the boy! I need my own discovery process. I need you on my team."

That is the type of support that I keep hearing girls ask for. They want to feel like it's safe to fully explore their identity. Sophia also rightfully pointed out to me that we are experiencing a new wave of feminism right now, which, thankfully, is a "You do you" type of radical love and cheering squad for all women and girls who want to express themselves beyond any and all systemic, constricting narratives. Sexual liberation is now joining hands with the many types of liberation that women yearn for.

In addition to all the lessons that Sophia so handily taught me, I have also come to learn that there is a level of identity-forming and exploration that happens when a teenage girl takes photos of herself. In later chapters, I'll expand on selfies and a teenage girl's contemplative abilities to analyze posts on social media, but these photos can be all things. There is no one-size-fits-all answer. It can be complicated, but *please don't underestimate a teenage girl's ability to have a conversation about it.* Growth and learning happen in an environment that's filled with respect and curiosity, not shame and judgment.

In listening to girls' thoughts on all these topics, I'm inspired to take this discussion further and pose some questions for all of us.

What if, sometimes, a teenage girl is indeed posting a sexy photo to grab the attention of her crush? I'm not saying if it's good or bad here, I'm simply challenging everyone to ask: What are we scared of?

Are you scared that she wants to have sex?

Are you scared that she might enjoy sex?

Are you scared that a boy is going to be so turned on that he tries to force her to have sex?

If you think she's too young to have sex, could you provide her with info that's helpful to her in processing her very-human desires?

If premarital sex is against your religion, have you considered that a teenage girl might think differently and is hiding it with shame?

Are you scared that secrets and shame might mess up her relationship with sex in the future?

Are you scared of her understanding the full power of her beauty and body?

Are you scared that she'll derive too much self-worth from being desired by her crush? What if her crush has been well educated in understanding and respectfully controlling their own sexual desire?

Is she not allowed to have the feeling of her crush desiring her? Do you consider that a bad thing? Why would that be bad?

These are the questions that have wildly inflamed my inner teenage girl. She's been confused for decades because she was taught a very basic, artificial fairy tale about romance. Man saves Woman, or Man completes Woman, or as 17-year-old Madelyn describes it:

"It's an identity rooted in being loved by a man."

However, modern-day teenage girls are no Sleeping Beauty. They have their eyes wide open. Madelyn expands on her thoughts:

"The fairy tale has been crushed. I would never expect a fairy tale because the reality around me is too obvious. All we can see is these boys who've been corrupted by their socialization, and these girls who seek validation from these corrupted boys, knowing the boys are corrupted, but still wanting their attention. Then, this prevents girls from finding their own divine femininity because they're searching for it outside of themselves. They're trying to fulfill the male gaze."

Wow, Sleeping Beauty is wide awake and wants so much more for her life than simply a kiss. This 17-year-old's powerful reflection empowers my inner teenage girl to stop searching outside herself, and start searching within . . . but for what?

This makes me think of a song beloved by the girls I spend time with, a song I've had so many arguments with adults about. Which is of course "WAP," Cardi B. and Megan Thee Stallion's "Wet-Ass Pussy." Teenage girls are absolutely confounded and disheartened that this song is so controversial. They do not understand why singing about a woman's sexual enjoyment is a bad thing. I'm going to go there with my questions again . . .

What is wrong with a vulva (turning to the biological term in the hopes that everyone will keep a mature, open mind) that is lubricating? A lubricated vulva is an indication of . . . *pleasure.*

Ah yes, now we're getting to the word that truly *terrifies.*

Nowhere, at any moment, in my sex education was "pleasure" a part of the conversation. Girls are not taught to look within, explore, and pursue their own understanding of what gives them pleasure. Why??? The media certainly permits teenage boys to have a goal of pleasure in their sexual exploration.

But a girl's pleasure? Now apparently, that's some scary shit.

So, yet again, we squash. We shove purity rings on girls' fingers and choose to criticize songs like "WAP" with a disgusted "What's the world come to?"

In all fairness, not every parent I know is fearful and resistant. A mom recently shared with me that her 18-year-old told her that she had sex for the first time, and the mom's first response was "Was it pleasurable? I hope so."

Wow, this is refreshingly new!

Unfortunately, the girl's reply was, "Not really."

So that's a bummer, but there's hope, because that mom helped her daughter sign up for a free sex-ed workshop that summer that focused on pleasure, which empowered her daughter to learn about her own body and get the answers she needed. A workshop like that is still rare, but I believe that leaning in to these conversations will help expand the possibilities. Clearly in that household, critical conversations around sex were openly and positively happening.

Woefully, what I'm usually witnessing is a culture that is vehemently avoiding conversations about a teenage girl's pleasure, for the sake of _____? Please, fill in the blank for me because I'm truly confused.

I've been unwrapping these mysteries for myself because only recently did I learn that sex isn't supposed to be painful. It took me until my thirties before I learned that I had a treatable medical condition that caused sex to be painful.

Why so long?

Shame.

Lack of education.

Sexist systems within the medical field.

And no one empowering me to seek sexual pleasure.

A tragedy for sure, and the teenage girl inside of me wants to start a revolution about it. She's harnessing both her pain and healing as a force to engage teenage girls just like her. She's expanding the conversation. She's asking ALL the questions. And she's making sure that pleasure is a part of every girl's sexual journey.

Do you want to join me? If so, then it's best to first check and make sure you're ready. I was flabbergasted by how much sexual shame I needed to unpack and heal first. In order to be a force for positive change, I had to start on a very personal and intimate level. It's hard to know how to support teenage girls in these difficult conversations if we can't even talk to ourselves about it. It requires a lot of questioning the "rules" that we've all been taught.

I recommend going back to the long list of questions earlier in this chapter and forcing yourself to have a personal reckoning with them.

Your answers will inform your own way forward. It can be hard to give explicit advice because liberating and embracing sexuality looks dramatically different for everyone. However, I'm hopeful that our collective healing around sex will tell a new story.

The teenage girls I spend time with love to discuss a much more expansive sexuality. Many of them identify as queer, finding their sexual identity no longer rooted in the attraction of a man. They're wisely refusing to be shamed for their appearance, and they're powerfully setting fire to any "rules" that have come before. Those burning rules are kindling for a dazzling new fire. The campfire I envisioned at the beginning of this chapter. Campfire sex is warm, loving, present, hot, connected, consensual, adventurous, and fun. It seeks authenticity, mutual respect, ease, and pleasure. It's what we should want for any person on this planet.

The way our society is right now, there is so much that's taboo to talk about sex, but instead, we really need to foster a space for teenage girls to be able to talk about their feelings around sexuality.

—NORA, AGE 18

---

✦ Rather than working to prevent and judge teenage girls' sexual choices, let's work to create a world that thoroughly educates everyone on sexual responsibility and pleasure.

✦ Judgment and control around girls' bodies, clothes, and sexuality create long-lasting shame that shuts down possibilities for open, necessary, and helpful conversations around sex.

✦ Sexual violence, objectification, and harassment are issues that people need to discuss openly and mindfully in order to solve the root causes, because currently, girls feel alone, blamed, and understandably angry in confronting these issues.

✦ If you feel uncomfortable talking about sex with your teenage girl, it's best to first ask yourself, "What is causing my discomfort?" If you don't interrogate yourself first, you risk passing along your own (understandable) wounds around difficult topics.

✦ The conversation is expanding around sexual liberation and how women and girls can explore their identity beyond constricting narratives and create a sense of agency in how they want to express themselves.

## CHAPTER FOUR

# PERFECTION

*Perfectionism is the belief that if we live perfect, look perfect,
and act perfect, we can minimize or avoid the pain of blame,
judgment, and shame. It's a shield. Perfectionism is a twenty-ton shield
that we lug around thinking it will protect us when, in fact, it's the
thing that's really preventing us from taking flight.*[1]

—Brené Brown

When I started working with teenage girls, I had no idea that dismantling their deeply entrenched relationship with perfection would become my full-time job. It is one of the most significant issues that I confront.

The subtle and overt demands on a girl to be perfect in all areas of her life start at a young age. I once complimented 11-year-old Mariana's handwriting and told her how much better it was than that of the student I had just worked with before her. She responded,

"Was it a boy? That would make sense, but if it's a girl, then she needs to get her act together!" She was offended by the idea that a girl might have bad handwriting, but a boy? Whatevs! In the world she knows, a girl MUST have perfect handwriting. Add "Perfect Handwriting" to the list of OBLIGATORY DEMANDS!

That is indeed the world wherein teenage girls are struggling. Cynthia is a 16-year-old with big opinions and an intellect to back them up. She works tirelessly to get perfect grades and holds herself to a standard that regards an A- as *failure*. She burns herself into a state of anxiety on a weekly basis, starting our sessions with monologues like:

"I haven't been working hard enough. Did I tell you that I have a 92.4 percent in English? It's not okay. I need to talk to the teacher about extra credit. I mean what if I don't get that grade up in time? Do you think they'll still allow me to go into AP Lit next year? If I don't get into AP, then Ivy League scholarships are off the table. Do you think I'll get into a good college? I've just been so overwhelmed, and I have a presentation tomorrow that I haven't memorized completely and what if I mess that up?"

And this is only the stress she's sharing with me out loud. I've learned that there's an even more tyrannical voice going on inside most teenage girls' heads, viciously directing her to beat herself up over *everything*. The domineering voice creates expectations of perfection that both paralyze and clobber her spirit. I watch this unrealistic standard set up a home inside her brain with a formidable neon sign above the door that screams "ANXIETY."

The National Institutes of Mental Health now reports that 38 percent of teenage girls have some type of anxiety disorder, more than any other age range or gender.[2]

I can deeply relate to how a teenage girl's performance-driven anxiety is wickedly paired with the pressure to be perfect. My parents' divorce threw a grenade into my teenage years, and I felt like I had to be the stabilizing force in the family. My parents didn't put that on me, but amid normal teenage angst and lacking tools to deal with life's trials, I lunged for what seemed like an obvious solution. *If I'm perfect enough, then I can control my future and avoid pain.* Rather than seeing how that's completely false and unreasonable, my psyche responded with destructive anxiety that flourished with worrying, overworking, controlling behaviors, dieting, setting impossible standards, obsessing over little things, people-pleasing, and never feeling like I was enough.

As an adult, I've been lucky enough to connect to teenage girls who've been the heroes who have helped liberate me from those patterns.

In witnessing and supporting their similar struggles, I finally began to learn the lesson that *perfection doesn't exist, and that self-compassion for my "flaws" is the only healthy way forward in a world saturated with uncertainty.*

Eighteen-year-old Fatima was just ending her first semester of college when she reached out to me in a panic. She had three late papers, and was certain that these papers were going to determine whether she passed two classes. The problem was that she could not get herself to write them. She was completely paralyzed. I knew that Fatima was not a girl who spent her semester partying. She's incredibly responsible and was on a vital, full-ride scholarship that would be threatened by failing a class.

After asking a lot of "why?"s and talking with her at length, we realized that her paralysis came from her feeling completely and utterly terrified of turning in a paper that wasn't worthy of an A. In high school, she would never have turned in less than A-quality work, and this level of perfection was deeply tied to her identity. She was also the first person in her family to go to college, so she was carrying a massive weight of pressure to succeed. She shared how she had been suffering from unrelenting migraines and stomach pain all semester. It was so intense that she had to go to the hospital several times.

Her level of stress had reached such dramatic heights that it was now affecting her physically. According to the American Psychological Association, teenagers report higher stress levels than adults, with 27 percent reporting levels at an 8, 9, or 10 on a 10-point scale, and 83 percent report that school is a significant stressor. Migraines, insomnia, and stomach pain are commonly reported physical symptoms of stress, while anxiety, irritability, and depression are the most common mental health implications.[3]

When a girl is as overwhelmed as Fatima, I know it's important to address the paralysis by breaking her process of dealing with it into steps. I might think that I know exactly what the right steps are, but it's crucial that I activate her choice in the process, asking questions along the lines of "What do you think the first step is? Do you want my guidance or advice on this? How do you want to handle this? How can I support you in this?"

She might have called me just to vent her feelings, so it's important for me to give her a choice. When dealing with an anxiety spiral, no amount of me telling her what to do will holistically help her in the long term.

If a girl invites me into her process, I make sure to emphasize that we can't go straight from Step 1 to Step 10. Even though we'd all love to, myself included. An immediate jump to Step 10 is the dazzling, false advertising campaign of PERFECTION. Unfortunately, this facade makes accomplishing Steps 4, 5, and 6 still feel like failure. In life, we usually exist within those mid-level steps.

Fatima determined that her first step was to ask her teachers for official extensions, letting them know about her physical health and hospital visits. She told me, "I don't even feel like I can show my face to them. I'm letting them down. I want them to think I'm perfect." More than writing the papers, she wanted my help in writing the emails to her teachers, because it was so incredibly scary for her to be vulnerable.

On top of breaking the process into steps, I try to expand a girl's options by permissioning her to solely exist in Steps 4, 5, and 6 and not even strive for Step 10. I ask, "What if you got a C? Or even a D, but at least you passed the class? Who cares? I don't care. I know how brilliant you are. You have nothing to prove. You can definitely turn in an imperfect paper. This grade doesn't define your worth."

When Cynthia (who shared her anxiety-monologue earlier) read a draft of this chapter, she highlighted these words that I told Fatima and commented beside them:

"This made me tear up . . . this is why you're writing the book, and it's going to make waves."

Fatima had a similar reaction. Not only did this idea of her grades not being her worth cause her to have an emotional response, but it also felt really controversial to her. I'm not sure if I'm making waves with the concept that *a grade is not a teenage girl's worth*, but if it is indeed provocative for you, then GREAT. The pressure of perfection on girls is leaving them paralyzed, physically ill, and anxiety ridden.

People regularly connect a girl's worth to her grades, making her feel like she always has something to prove. It blows a girl's mind when I don't reinforce that, because it feels like all she has ever experienced is the pressure to be perfect.

To be clear, I'm not saying let's make girls mediocre. I've never seen that outcome in response to reduced academic pressure. I'm addressing how we can silence the blaring noise of perfection because it's harshly affecting a girl's mental health. She feels a lot more cared about as a human being when I explicitly make the distinction that she has nothing to prove. And in terms of problem-solving, I find that this type of "Who cares?" permissioning helps relax her brain so that more options can appear. She can find better solutions when she's not suffocating in fear.

I use the word *permissioning* rather than "I give her permission to" because it's not about my specific permission, but rather a larger, societal permissioning. I'm trying to create a liberated space for a girl to step outside the bounds of "perfection," where she has permission to make mistakes and exist happily and healthily on a different step, other than Step 10.

A few weeks later, Fatima told me that she got a B- and B in the classes. I was shocked to learn how well she did because she had told me that her papers were not good, and she still thought she could fail. I had a moment of reckoning with her where I pointed out that she wasn't even close to failing. I acknowledged her feelings around the situation, but we made sure to discuss how perfectionism drastically warped her perception of her classwork. Since Fatima fell short of her standard of perfection, she had given herself no choice but to feel shitty about herself. Even though it wasn't reality, her emotional experience had been entirely one of failure.

Expecting perfection of oneself perpetuates a state of fear. Fear creates anxiety. Anxiety is destructive. It's that simple.

The researched fact is that between the ages of 12 and 13, the percentage of girls who feel the pressure to be perfect rises from 35 to 51 percent, which is more than half of all 13-year-olds![4] Within this discussion, I'm encouraging parents and others to intervene at an earlier point in a girl's life with the tools to help her learn the candid truth that life is full of challenges and that we are undoubtedly going to swim in what I call a mud pool of mistakes. AND THAT'S OKAY.

In my work with teenage girls, I've learned a lot about the "mistakes" and "flaws" that make us feel like failures. Girls love to quickly latch on to black-and-white binaries, such as their being "good" or "bad" at math. There is rarely any room for the in-between when they first start working on a problem and make some mistakes.

The zone where I see *learning* take place is where the extremes of black and white mix, creating a "gray zone." I'm constantly encouraging them to "embrace the gray," because it's hard to learn something without first making a few mistakes. Those mistakes lead to learning, and that learning leads to growth. An allegiance to "perfection" thwarts this process by sending a girl's brain into an anxiety spiral.

The anxiety spiral usually includes destructive self-talk happening inside her mind that will be addressed with helpful strategies in the chapter Self-Doubt. Something that a parent can do to bring attention to the gray zone is to simply point out binary thinking when it happens.

I say to girls, "I noticed you're using words like 'good' or 'bad.' 'Perfect' or 'failure.' 'Hard' or 'easy.' 'Hate it' or 'love it.' For me, it's become unhealthy to live in those extremes. I close myself off to so many options when I think something can only be two things. There is so much magic that exists between all that."

When a girl hears that her parents are content with her being in the gray zone, it inspires flexibility, experimentation, curiosity, and trust in the evolving process. Without that breathing room, a girl finds herself in a state of shame when she doesn't perform perfectly, which perpetuates the cycle of thinking:

"Next time, I'll be perfect, which will make me stop feeling horrible like this."

But that's not what's going to happen, because *perfection doesn't exist.*

Another way to break up binary thinking is by asking questions with percent answers. If I ask a girl if she is understanding something, she'll often reply with a simple "yeah" or "not really," which is rarely accurate. Instead, I ask:

"What percent are you understanding this? With one hundred percent being you completely understand and zero percent being you completely don't understand?"

Girls usually spend a lot more time thinking of this answer, and I'll often get something in the 50 to 89 percent zone. This is the gray zone!

With this framework, we can laser into the parts of the material that she's still not understanding. This approach dismantles the idea that we immediately and perfectly understand everything right from the beginning, and instead, it creates the much-needed space to actually learn. Similar to the mid-level steps that I walked Fatima through.

I make sure to tell girls that the dazzling glare of a Step 10 "success" can be blinding. Even people who've seemed to hit Step 10 in their career (like winning an Oscar or becoming CEO), immediately go in search of a new step to place in front of them. The pursuit of perfection is never-ending.

I've had girls argue with me that earning 100 percent on a test is perfection, but I point out that it's a fleeting, transitory type of "perfection." It's not something you can hold on to—it will inevitably slip away. There's always another test, and the 100 is usually gone so quickly that we're left clinging to nothing. That type of short-term high is not something that will make anyone feel continuously good and whole inside.

Alternatively, I point out how perfectionism's deeper patterns are connected to our feelings of worth. The faulty idea that perfection creates our worthiness when it comes to being loved.

A test score isn't going to love you, but a parent might show more love in response to a good grade. Of course, it's obviously problematic to connect love to success on a test, but I see it happening *all the time*. Most parents aren't even conscious they are doing it.

Parents affirm the pursuit of perfection, a lot. Even when they try not to. Even if they're aware of the problematic nature of doing so. I see it occur incessantly, as if it were the doctor banging that little hammer against your knee to test your reflexes. The knee pops up whether you want it to or not.

When a kid is successful, it reflects well on the parents, which triggers the parents' need to look perfect as well. I'm going to be bold and say that every single human is playing out some type of internal battle with their relationship to "perfection," whether they know it or not. It often doesn't show up in every aspect of someone's life, but it'll manage to wiggle its way in.

With parents, I often see the same narrative surrounding our deep need for worthiness. The idea that if I have a perfect and successful kid, then I've done something good, and that goodness makes me feel worthy of love and admiration. I say this without judgment. I believe that every human struggles with this sense of worthiness.

Additionally, parents often unconsciously create competition between siblings around this issue of success. They might try to motivate their daughter to do better in math by praising the other sibling's high math grades, or tell their daughter to go get help with her math homework from her older brother. I know parents' intentions are good, and I understand them wanting their kid to succeed in school, but if you ask a teenage girl how she feels about it, she will tell you, "My parents like my brother more than me because he's smarter." This more deeply translates into: my parents' love and attention are conditional around academic success. Instead, a parent could ask the girl, "What do you think is the best solution to help you in math right now? Do you want to get help from your brother?"

If she turns down the idea, then maybe ask her with a lot of sincerity and care, "Do you want your math grade to get better?" Sometimes that needs to be the starting point. If she says no, I would lean in fully and put the ball in her court, which she probably won't expect, saying, "Okay, then I'll let you handle it how you want. But would it be okay if I check in with you again about it in a month?"

If you intentionally say that you're letting her handle it, you might be surprised how she steps up to take responsibility. But I also like leaving the option open to bring it up again—an option that she agrees to. Adding pressure isn't going to get her grade higher. Or if pressure does seem to raise her grade, please know that she's very likely not going to feel healthy in the process of getting there. If she says that she does want the grade higher, then you could ask with a loving tone, "What's holding you back? Is there fear of not doing it perfectly?"

It's so important to meet her where she's at, which might be a Step 4 or 5, rather than solely driving hard toward a "perfect" 10. Perfection can not only be paralyzing but also push a girl to burn out.

When I asked 15-year-old Giselle about her thoughts on perfection, she specifically commented on not only competition with siblings but also with other girls:

"People like to compare and pit girls against each other. It feels crushing because I already have pretty high standards for myself and now I have to factor in another girl's standard? When more pressure is added, it makes me feel burnt out."

When I see parents trying to motivate their daughters with competition, it almost always has the reverse effect. It makes them want to give up or sends them spiraling into anxiety. The goal of perfection is already beating a very loud drum inside their head, and unnecessary competition is often the bang that breaks the drum.

I know it can be such a hard balance to strike, but I find that a girl's mental health improves when a parent says, "Did you try your best? That's all I care about." Or if she gets a C, they ask, "How does it make you feel? I know how hard you worked. Are you okay with it?" If she's not, just hold space for her feelings. I can't tell you how many times I see a girl terrified to tell her parents that she got a B on a test. She doesn't need the extra weight of her parents' opinion, which she will feel as disappointment and judgment. She just needs to know that you're on her team and that you trust her to make good decisions. From my experience, if a girl is doing really badly in school, that just means more loving curiosity needs to happen. Not more pressure. This isn't always a home issue, so it's important that other adults like coaches and teachers also implement an approach that leads with care.

Some of my greatest wins have come from swimming around in the space where I shift a girl's focus away from perfection, and instead, toward embracing and reframing imperfection. For me, "mistakes" and "flaws" are bright shining pieces of information that make a person unique. That uniqueness is the key to their success.

I was working on writing an essay with 13-year-old Nina, who was nervously darting her eyes around as she struggled with self-doubt. That day, her eyes were filled with anxiety around the writing process because she kept writing run-on sentences and losing her train of thought. I asked her to put into words what it felt like inside her head, and she called it a "swirl." I responded with a big smile, "Perfect! We'll call this the Nina Swirl then!"

Nina arched her eyebrows, weirded out by my enthusiasm for her "flaw."

Over many years of diving into the mud pool of mistakes, I've found that naming and taking ownership of a "flaw," in a lighthearted way, takes away its power to negatively impact us. Since that moment with Nina, we have completely changed the energy around her Nina Swirl. When it happens, I often lovingly singsong "Nina Swirl!" and Nina laughs wholeheartedly. That laughter puts her brain and anxiety at ease. She doesn't feel like something is wrong with her. Instead, she feels like she understands her own brain better, and she feels more at peace with who she is. There is warmth around her identity, and the feeling of *I am enough* fills her heart.

It's important to note that owning her swirl with levity, instead of judging it, gives Nina the gray-zone space to explore it. Laughter and levity are a critical part of the process. I make sure to laugh at myself all the time when I'm working with teenage girls, because laughter is the enemy of perfectionism. It's very difficult to anxiously worry or judge yourself when you're laughing. A little moment of laughter offers me a portal into a place of ease, and ease is where growth can happen.

Wonderfully, Nina has now figured out how to "harness her swirl" as we call it. She can recognize when it's happening and navigate it with a mindfulness that leads her to better writing. Basically, we used her uniqueness or "flaw" to find her natural flow. Sometimes a girl just needs to sit with who she is, explore it, and find some peace around it. Giving her that space to explore will be expanded upon in the identity chapter, but it's important to note that we didn't try to stuff Nina into a "perfect" box of essay writing because the truth is, no one fits in that box. There's a lot more magic to be discovered by doing a cannonball into the mud-pool and realizing that mud can be a really fun thing to play in.

Perfectionism can rear its ugly head in varied and hidden ways, but I'd say the demand for perfection in our looks (body, clothes, hair, makeup, weight, etc.) is one of the more treacherous war zones women face—and the first grenades usually explode during the teenage years. I find that a girl's eating habits are where the anxiety and pursuit of perfection veer toward the extreme.

Eating disorders among teenage girls are so pervasive that when I sit down to brainstorm the classic college essay on overcoming an obstacle, 95 percent of the time I ask, "Do you want to bring up your eating disorder at all?"

And then the girl worries about the idea being too cliché because every girl she knows has struggled with some type of disordered eating.

Can we just pause for a moment and recognize the severity of that statement?

Pointing out its commonality is in no way an attempt to minimize the severity of the issue. Anorexia is currently the deadliest mental health disorder that exists. The anorexia mortality rate of 5.86 percent is dramatically higher than even schizophrenia (2.5 percent), bipolar disorder (2.1 percent), or depression (1.6 percent).[5]

Body image permeates all the topics in this book and will be covered more thoroughly in the chapter Beauty, but I believe that we've completely underestimated the impact perfectionism has on our eating habits and self-image. Teenage girls have a long list of things they hate about their bodies. And when I've asked a girl what she likes about her body, she can barely name one thing. This situation didn't start at birth. Years of socialization and cultural messaging have created this monstrous anxiety around what a "perfect" body "should" look like.

On the other side of the coin, teenage girls usually love to talk about fashion, makeup, hair, and looks, so I've had to find a balance between caring and connecting versus perpetuating the harmful narratives around some unobtainable ideal. And I try to be conscious and recognize when I myself have been sucked into the very same narrative.

At the recommendation of a 16-year-old fashionista and makeup tutorial expert, Zandy, I decided to get a spray tan in preparation for a fancy wedding I was attending. It was a luxury to spend money on something like this, but the never-ending demands of perfection that wailed from my pale skin were begging me to do it.

However, the morning after getting it, I looked in the mirror with hopeful eyes only to see wild streaks across my neck and chest. I was horrified because there is something worse than looking bad—looking like you tried waaaay too hard to look good, but still ended up looking bad. The wedding was that afternoon, so there was no time to repair this orange-brown modern art that marred my body. I texted Zandy to tell her the tragedy, and she responded with:

"Oh noooo. I wouldn't go!" That struck me right away as pretty drastic. I was rattled that she would choose to miss a friend's wedding because of how she looked. I had already traveled with a dress that bared skin, so I had no choice but to dive headfirst into the discomfort of imperfection.

Yet, when the women at the wedding took in the sight of my glowing menagerie of patterned skin tones, my anxiety was quickly swept away with loving smiles and playful giggles as they assured me:

"I've been there."

"Aw, we love you."

"You look great. That dress is killer."

"The beauty industry is such bullshit. Who cares!"

They didn't try to usher me into the bathroom and fix me. With loving acceptance, they let me be me in all my messy tan humanness. The rest of the night was filled with tons of laughter and authentic connection as I leaned in more and more to the honesty of a silly mistake. That's all it was—a mistake. And by tearing away the social lens that my body needed to look "perfect," the mistake actually was really nothing but hilarious.

Over the years, I've learned that people don't like "perfect" people. They're uncomfortable to be around because we feel like if they're judging themselves by such high standards, then they're probably judging us, too. They also come off as fake because we all know it's impossible to be perfect. We're left imagining what that person's dark secrets are. This creates a lack of trust and blocks people from deeply connecting. After telling 18-year-old Nora this story, she shared her conclusions:

"If people are trying to act perfect, you don't get to the realness of them, you don't get to any of the substance of who they are. It's ultimately really difficult to form real connections with people if you're trying to be perfect. And it's not sustainable."

When I told Zandy about the wedding, she was quiet for a moment before saying:

"That's so cool it didn't matter and you were able to connect with people about it. By not going, I would have missed out on that." I assured her that her revelation was quite wise. She was seeing how her choice to avoid being viewed as imperfect would have kept her from a lot of laughter and human connection. And now she knows that she'll make a different choice in the future.

Teenage girls are good at acknowledging when they've learned something. Adults are so often stuck in their ways that it takes a lot of pain before anyone starts admitting they're wrong. By embracing the gray zone, teenage girls have taught me how to harness the powerful force of intellectual and emotional growth.

Additionally, in order to find the joy of swimming in that mud pool, I've learned to embrace the practice of self-compassion. This is not a new and revolutionary solution, but rather one that's thankfully been getting more attention in the last decade. In particular, Stanford Medicine's Center for Compassion and Altruism Research and Education (CCARE) largely highlights the work of Dr. Kristin Neff to define this expanding practice. One of the definitions offered from her research is:

"Self-compassion involves being kind to oneself when confronting personal inadequacies or situational difficulties, framing the imperfection of life in terms of common humanity, and being mindful of negative emotions so that one neither suppresses nor ruminates on them."[6]

My time spent exploring "flaws" with teenage girls has certainly been a time that I could characterize as sharing our "common humanity" together. When girls share their mistakes with me, I often say, "Yeah, that happens, you're human."

And then I share a mistake of my own, so that she knows I'm human too. We might feel bummed together for a moment about our mistakes, but then we often end up laughing about them. From that definition of self-compassion, the emphasis on *common* humanity resonates with me because no one wants to feel alone in their imperfection.

Dr. Neff offers a link on her website to "Test How Self-Compassionate You Are."[7] I've found it to be a really helpful tool with girls to spark self-awareness around their relationship to perfectionism and self-compassion. But very interestingly, girls are always so nervous to take the test because they tell me that they're so scared of failing or doing badly on the "test." Which, of course, is all the more reason to take it. Their discomfort with the test really inspires some depth-filled discussions.

When we're not clinging to the facade of perfection, we're left with a lot of feelings of discomfort and uncertainty. Those are the feelings that push us to grow. Those are the moments when I see a girl's wisdom gain power and point us in a new, healthier direction. In contrast, anxiety spiraling into mental and physical stress disorders is an exquisite model for how perfectionism ravages our headspace and well-being.

Witnessing how teenage girls embrace discomfort and adopt

self-compassion can help us all feel powerful in owning that space, but it's best if the shift starts at a young age.

When my niece Junia was six, I noticed that she was obsessed with constructing her Lego sets *perfectly* in accordance with the directions and would experience extreme frustration if one little thing went wrong. Gently and steadily, I began to message to her that mistakes happen and that there's no "perfect" way to do something. I made sure to intentionally break some of the "rules" of activities and express enthusiasm for imperfections. I didn't know how much it had sunk in until one day, my brother accidentally took a wrong turn while driving, exclaiming with annoyance, "Things are not going perfectly today!"

That's when Junia, sitting in her car seat, chimed in, "Dad, perfect doesn't exist. It'll be okay."

We cannot underestimate how much girls are absorbing at a young age. Our words and choices matter because they create a model for kids to follow. We can break the cycles that no longer serve us. When I asked two 13-year-olds about the messaging they wish girls would hear earlier and more often, they said:

"It's really helpful to hear that everybody makes mistakes, like literally everybody."

"Yeah, you can learn from mistakes, they make you a better person."

"We grow from mistakes."

The wisdom of these girls gives me hope that we can evolve. We can let go of old stories and actively choose a story that embraces our full, imperfect humanity.

Perfection is an evil in disguise that buries you in blankets of worry and interest in your improvement, but ultimately those blankets smother you.

—CYNTHIA, AGE 16

---

+ Expectations of perfection and binary thinking block exploration, innovation, and the overall learning process.

+ Reframing your "flaws" helps you celebrate and embrace your uniqueness.

+ Your grades/job/wealth/kids/successes are not your worth. You have inherent value, no matter what you accomplish.

+ Self-compassion helps alleviate feelings of unworthiness because it embraces the truth that all human beings are imperfect.

+ Uncertainty is uncomfortable, but seeking to control and avoid pain by being "perfect" will not leave you feeling whole and at peace, because perfection doesn't exist.

## CHAPTER FIVE

# PEOPLE-PLEASING

*Whatever culture, whatever country, girls are taught
to please others as opposed to pleasing themselves.*[1]
—V (formerly Eve Ensler)

I t's fine."

"Really?"

"Yeah . . . yeah, it's fine."

Fifteen-year-old Lucia stared at me with her large brown eyes. Normally full of ideas and excitement, these eyes look empty and defeated. She's telling me everything is "fine" in order to make me feel comfortable.

School was not going well for Lucia. Additionally, her family's health and childcare needs were falling on her shoulders. It was clearly a burden that, in an ideal world, would not be her responsibility, but life is rarely ideal. What killed me in this moment was that she was prioritizing my comfort, my needs, above her own, making sure that I felt "fine," even while she was clearly in pain.

People-pleasing is ferociously sneaky in how it bares its teeth. For teenage girls, it can look like a smile, but in reality, so many of her facial muscles are tensely clenching, trying to hold it all together. A study from Girls Inc. found that 74 percent of girls say "they are under a lot of pressure to please everyone."[2] I see girls from all different backgrounds shouldering an emotional burden within a family dynamic.

It slithers its way into so many facets of a girl's life until it's absolutely normalized. "It's fine" might not be as blatant as the people-pleasing classics like forced laughter, endless giving of one's time and attention, overcompensating, manufactured enthusiasm, and overdone politeness that we all know so well, but it's just as insidious.

I relate so deeply, because every day I still agonize over how much or how little I should care about making other people happy. Teenage girls have brought it to my awareness and now I must reckon with it— the root cause, the *why*, and where do we go from here?

In order to avoid even the potential of tension and conflict, girls have been taught to people-please. As much as a girl will unleash her fury at her parents in the privacy of her home, out in the world, she can slap on a smile with the grace of a champion ready to win gold at the Niceness Olympics.

If a little girl, ages three to eleven, is found to be annoying, aggressive, bossy, loud, or demanding, she is thoroughly and often severely "corrected" with a tone that penetrates her psyche for a lifetime. Little girls learn very quickly that they need to be sweet, charming, humble, polite, and thoughtful in order to get positive attention and succeed in this world. And as they grow into women, they learn each subsequent lesson along this people-pleasing path. In many workplaces, a show of assertiveness from a woman can quickly get her thrown into the "bitch" category, so she needs to make moves very cautiously and amiably, in order to not threaten the professional patriarchy. Quite simply, we're taught that our best bet to succeed in life is to not only be "perfect," as already noted, but also to be . . . likable.

Women and girls learn how to perform our gender within the framework of perfection by making sure that everyone around us is happy and comfortable, even if we ourselves are not. I see this show up in the most common word that I hear from a teenage girl's mouth: *Sorry.*

Teenage girls say "sorry" about *everything*. It's the word that covers all unforeseen potentials, so she won't offend or say something wrong, guaranteeing that she will be viewed as pleasing. This type of "sorry" is very different from a heartfelt apology, which will be expanded upon later. This "sorry" sounds like an empty flurry of words, and after spending so much time with teenage girls, I realized that I say it a lot too! I ended up telling girls that I wanted to stop saying it so much, and I asked them if they would point it out when I do it. Most of them responded with:

"Oh my gosh I do it too! Let's do it together!" And to my delight, we all started catching ourselves saying the most unnecessary "sorrys," and we began changing the habit. However, if a girl is having a hard time stopping the stream of "sorrys," I recommend asking her in a nonjudgmental tone:

"Why do you think you're saying sorry?" Some of the answers I've heard from girls include:

"I feel like I'm never doing anything right," "I don't want to disappoint people," and "I just want everyone to be happy." With those harder-to-hear answers, I'll usually pause and uncomfortably sit with where these messages could be coming from. Then I'll lovingly ask:

"Have I done anything to make you feel like that?"

A question like this can open up the possibility for a much deeper level of connection. It's where honesty develops and trust blossoms.

The enemy of this space is defensiveness.

Receiving and holding space for these types of feelings, ones where I might be personally involved in the hurt, is a space where I can give her the gift of feeling heard and understood. It's a space for healing.

If the conversation is on the simpler side and a girl is shutting down a lot of the questions, I often go back to the basics of asking what she wants:

"Do you want to stop saying these types of sorrys?" Near the end of these kinds of conversations, I always like to finish on a note of agreeing with her and empowering her sense of agency:

"Okay, sounds good. I'll let you handle it in the way that feels good for you."

No matter what, I'm always trying to create a safe environment where we both can be more intentional and authentic with our language.

The other blaring-alarm word is *fine*. No one actually wants to be fine. They want to be happy or great. Even "good" is better than "fine." I've asked teenage girls what they really mean when they say it, and they told me that the secret subtext is:

"I'm surviving," "I'm getting through it," "I can handle it," "I'll ultimately be okay, but right now I feel like shit."

There's a sneaky lesson taught to girls at a young age that if they show they're upset or "get emotional," then it'll just make a bad situation worse. And if they're making something harder, then people won't like them. If people don't like them, then they won't be happy or succeed.

"Fine" tells the world not to worry about them. Because if people are worrying about them, then they must not be perfect and likable.

"Fine" is usually a girl's tagline right after telling me some type of horror story that's playing out in her life. I've heard stories of childhood molestation, racist comments from teachers, a rageaholic parent losing it on them, a sibling being hospitalized for anorexia, a volleyball coach fired for sexual harassment, a parent losing a job and now the family is facing eviction . . . all concluded with "But it's fine."

That's when I say, "It's not fine."

She's usually very surprised by this response. I continue with, "That sounds awful. You don't need to make me feel better about it. I can look honestly at it with you, if you want. You don't have to endure this alone."

I explain how I don't want her to label that behavior/situation/event as "fine" because then it's normalized and accepted. Before learning how alone a teenage girl can feel in moments like these, I used to react differently. In the past, I found that I tried to quickly get rid of my own discomfort by saying, "It'll get better," or "Let's look on the bright side," or "At least it's not . . ."

But none of those are teaching her what is and isn't "fine." Instead, it's minimizing her experience and teaching her to sacrifice her honesty and well-being for the sake of my comfort. By forcing "positivity" onto her story, I'm reinforcing the idea that other people's needs should come before her own.

So instead, using the tools of holding space for feelings, phrasing everything as a question, and giving her a choice, I ask:

"What do you need to feel supported? What do you need in order to feel safe in recognizing that this situation isn't fine? I know that you'll ultimately be okay, but are there any feelings you need to vent? Let's think about your needs right now."

This is when I see her eyes soften, sometimes fill with tears, and her body relax. She finally feels safe to open up and share her truth—a truth that, if it remains hidden, can turn into a whole lot of unhealthy patterns.

"It's fine" is a state of tension and bracing for impact. It's a mask that not only teenage girls put on in order to power through but maybe we all put on this mask? I know I certainly do.

Now, when I decide to consciously acknowledge "It's NOT fine," my spirit relaxes into a state of honesty, and I'm able to ask for the care and support that I so desperately need.

For most of us, exorcizing people-pleasing habits may be not only a journey of confronting our unmet needs but also of finding freedom from other people's approval.

I regularly discuss with teenage girls internal vs. external validation—whether they're aiming for good grades to make their parents happy or to make themselves happy. A concept that their brains understand pretty easily, but in practice, it's a whole other game. This need for approval also shows up in the frequent concern:

"I don't think my teacher likes me."

Teenage girls talk a lot about whether their teacher likes them or not. They tie it to their potential to succeed in the class or if they even like the class.

Worrying about if someone likes them is a bomb that detonates during this time of life, as it's been found that girls' confidence in people liking them drops from 71 to 38 percent between their tween and teen years.[3] This seemingly never-ending worry is a dead end when it comes to feeling whole and fulfilled, because no matter how hard they try, teenage girls cannot control whether someone likes them. And I'll repeat that for every other human being on the planet. *We can't control whether someone likes us.*

"But they'll think I'm mean." "But they'll think I'm annoying." "But they'll think I'm being difficult." "But they'll think I'm dumb."

Girls tell me these things all the time. And so do grown adults. Reflecting on the amount of energy that we all expend on worrying about what other people might think of us, well, I think we can all collectively agree on a big "YIKES." It's a monstrous amount of (wasted) time and energy.

Last I checked, no one has magical powers to control another person's thoughts, right? Because if you do, please let me know, and I'll happily recant and join your magical team. I mean, sure, we can *manipulate* people, sometimes finding "success" in getting them to think what we want. However, my guess is that it won't feel sustainable or fulfilling to walk that path. Considering the complex world of each human being's brain, it seems safe to say that it's *impossible* to travel inside the mind of another person and know what they're truly thinking, and then control it.

In place of that, we experience perceived control. A concept of control that comes back to the idea of "If I'm perfect enough, then people will like me, I'll feel safe, and I'll be okay in life." It's an attempt to earn love that's rooted in fear.

I've learned over the years that telling girls not to worry about whether people like them with some upbeat positivity doesn't really work. I've had to be more blunt, directing the focus back to the girl herself, telling her:

"Pleasing other people is a never-ending cycle that won't make you happy. Only *you* can determine what will make you happy."

This creates a pause that brings the girl back to her own heart. She has to spend some legitimate time thinking about what makes her happy. Now, of course, I'm not against good grades, kindness, thoughtfulness, generosity, etc.—qualities that are considered pleasing—but there needs to be a much more nuanced conversation around authenticity and how much we really perform in the pursuit of other people's approval, versus our own.

Girls often respond to the idea of making themselves happy with "But that's kind of selfish, right?"

So then I ask, "Couldn't seeking everyone's approval be considered selfish too? I think of it as me manipulating them to like me, so that I feel good about myself."

I always try to implicate myself in these conversations. I usually share vulnerably that sometimes I only have warm, happy feelings if my good actions are being acknowledged and affirmed by others. I don't think it's bad to feel good about those things, but unless those actions are also authentically aligned with my own heart, then I'm giving other people power over me. By depending on their approval, I'm giving them the power to control my happiness.

This brings me to the significant people-pleasing lesson I've learned from teenage girls: *The only person who I can truly please is (drumroll) . . . myself.*

If I end up pleasing other people, it will be because I happen to match *their* standard—*their* barometer of what makes *them* happy. I place the control in *their* hands. Yes, sometimes what makes another person happy also happens to make me happy, but I'm focusing on the moments of discord, which can be very sly.

For example, 15-year-old Marli is a fantastic volleyball player. Her mom couldn't be prouder that her daughter made the varsity team as a freshman. She herself was also a star volleyball player in high school, and it's so fun for her to see her daughter following in her footsteps. But lately, Marli has felt the mounting intensity, including the stress of the six-times-a-week practices, missing school for games, her mom's competitive pressure, and the weight of colleges potentially scouting her. Marli also keeps getting minor injuries while playing and is enduring regular migraines.

I decided to ask Marli if she actually likes playing volleyball. She paused for a moment while she thought about it, then answered: "I like being good at it."

"Yeah, you're great at it. Anything else you like?"

"It makes my mom happy. We can bond over it."

As usual, a teenage girl's inner wisdom highlights the truth. I lean into the moment. "But do you actually like it? Or are you playing volleyball to make your mom happy?"

Marli's eyes widen with awareness.

"Oh shit."

"What would you really love to do with your time instead? If you didn't have to play volleyball all the time?"

"I mean, I like volleyball. It's fine, I'm good at it. It'll be good for college."

"Right . . . but close your eyes and listen to your heart right now. Not the voice of anyone else. Only you. What would you *love* to be doing with your time?"

Marli closes her eyes and pauses. She looks a bit uncomfortable, but after a moment, she utters quietly, "I love fashion design. I have so many ideas that I draw in a sketchbook when I'm on the bus to games."

"Oh cool! I know about a good sewing class on the weekends. Would that interest you?"

"Oh my gosh, yes!!!"

It's important to recognize how a teenage girl's unconscious desire to please her mom led her down a specific path. Soon after this, Marli actually ended up quitting volleyball, explaining to her mom that she wasn't really enjoying it and was doing it for the wrong reasons, which her mom thankfully understood and supported. Marli invested tons of time into fashion design, as rigorously as she did volleyball, but her stress and migraines went away. Spending time doing what she authentically loves has helped her blossom into a happier, healthier young woman every day. Marli even told me, "I feel more powerful being able to spend time doing what I love rather than what I think I *should* be doing."

She feels "powerful" when she's making choices that please herself.

I hear soooo many versions of Marli's story in my work with teenage girls. It happens a lot, specifically with sports, because there's often a lineage of familial investment in a particular sport that (understandably) influences a kid. But I find that so many parents have forgotten to ask their kid if they love it. They assume that a kid being good at something is proof enough that they should be pursuing it.

Unfortunately, the act of making another person happy, is often the thing that tricks the person into feeling happy about it, rather than the thing itself.

This can only continue for so long without it ultimately causing some type of pain, which I've seen exhibit itself mentally, emotionally, physically, subtly, or explosively. Feeling separation from one's authenticity eventually piles up. I've deeply learned from teenage girls how to recognize a disconnection from one's authentic self and how to address it. I'll explore the process more in the identity chapter, but for right now, I want to emphasize how an identity of "selflessness" so often permeates women's experiences.

While brainstorming a historical essay on women with 13-year-old Bella, I asked her for words she would use to describe women.

Playing with her dark brown hair as she reflected, she sighed heavily and said, "Selfless. But I'm not sure if that's a good thing."

Ah yes, the classic female martyr, always taking care of everyone else's needs before her own, and going the extra mile to make sure everyone is happy. The pattern can show up in the workplace—handling the coworker's birthday cake, offering to take meeting notes, taking on extra work. It can show up in larger family dynamics—hosting the holidays, securing care for an aging parent, mediating arguments, planning everyone's travel. And then of course, the mother martyr is a tale as old as time—cooking, washing dishes, monitoring schoolwork, cleaning the house, organizing extracurriculars, sacrificing everything for her children's well-being, and carrying out unpaid labor for all of history.

Sure, women can enjoy these tasks and actively choose them, which is great. But also, the pattern of women's martyrdom and selflessness is so omnipresent that it needs to be acknowledged for its obvious connection to people-pleasing.

When a woman does these things, she is most often pleasing another person ahead of and instead of herself.

And teenage girls watch their mom modeling this behavior *all the time.* I see girls absorb so many of the same patterns. It could be as simple as an overexplaining text message when she needs to cancel a tutoring session that's filled with tons of nice words, long excuses, exclamation points, and "sorrys." A mother's and daughter's texts to me on these matters are usually very similar. Communication like this signifies that they are uncomfortable with saying something that is not ideal, because they're scared of me not being happy about it. Their overly nice texts are supposed to make me feel better, but if I'm being honest, they just make me feel like I need to make them feel better about the cancellation. I always feel compelled to respond with:

"No worries!" "All good!" "No problem!"

Even if their cancellation totally messed up my day. Because I also need to feel like they're happy with me. I know everyone's intentions are kind in this scenario, but I also think this pattern is holding us all back, wasting a lot of unnecessary energy. It's an inauthentic, people-pleasing performance that we all know well and are clearly handing down to the next generation. When teenage boys text me about a tutoring cancellation, it's usually pretty simple—"I'm so sorry, but I have to cancel today. The cancellation fee is okay. Can we reschedule for this weekend?" It's still respectful and considerate, but I'm not fielding his stress about the situation to the point that I need to make him feel better about it. Instead, I can respond with a simple "Thanks, yes, how about Sunday at 11 a.m.?"

Figuring out how to keep a pleasing tone in my texts can be exhausting. But I still participate in the dynamic. Even when a woman friend texts me with a simple "ok," I can spiral into silly thinking that maybe she's mad at me.

It all comes back to unpleasant feelings.

I have a complete and utter aversion to the feeling of being displeasing. The thought of someone not liking me . . . hurts. It hurts to feel it. So, I'd rather put on a dazzling performance of positivity in order to distract. But this disconnection from my feelings doesn't make me feel better. It makes me feel tense.

Imagine the women you know who are really intense people-pleasers. You might think of them as nice, but aren't they also kind of annoying? There's a tension I feel when they're trying a little too hard to make me happy, almost like trying to control my perception of them, and then at the same time, they're sacrificing their own well-being. I don't want that. I want them to be happy and healthy too.

It's the classic airplane analogy that we need to put on our own oxygen mask before we help a child put on theirs. I wish the flight attendant would be a little more explicit about it all, something like, "If you put on the child's oxygen mask before your own, YOU WILL DIE, do you understand? You'll run out of oxygen, fall forward, knock your head against your tray table, and your unconscious body will crumple into that teeny-tiny legroom space. Your child will NOT be able to help you then, so basically your efforts to be selfless *will kill you*."

Then this audacious flight attendant will proceed to give a pep talk about women's universal struggle to overcome people-pleasing martyrdom. Passengers will get emotional and lives will be changed.

Book me on this airline!!!

I often think that the trapped scream inside of teenage girls comes from not only a desperate need to be imperfect (a.k.a. human) but also a fierce need to be displeasing. That's right, we *need* to be displeasing sometimes. We need space to be broken, annoyed, angry, frustrated, moody, and . . . unlikable.

We all need a safe space to connect with these types of feelings. I often tell girls that they can be mad at me. When I give them a deadline or assignment they don't like, I let them know that they can be annoyed with me. I can handle their displeasing feelings.

I've also messed up along the way and have rightfully deserved their annoyance and anger. While I usually always ask a girl's permission before sharing something with her parents, one time I shared with 14-year-old Emma's parents that her essay writing wasn't going well, and her parents got so mad at her. In a moment of overreaction, they blamed her for not working hard enough and set tons of new homework rules. I hadn't intended for them to take such drastic action, but they did. I couldn't have foreseen that type of reaction, but guess who could have? Emma. I should have talked about it with her first—shared my concerns about her essay writing and asked her directly what would be helpful in trying to improve it. Having her stressed-out parents implement helicoptering oversight was definitely not helpful.

Emma was upset about her parents' reaction, but I noticed that she didn't want me to feel bad about it. She knew that I didn't have bad intentions, which I appreciated, because I did feel awful about it, but I wanted to make room for her feelings as well.

"It's okay to be upset with me. I messed up and should have talked with you about this first. Tell me about your annoyance and anger with the situation. I can handle it."

In this moment, I'm attempting to refocus care and attention on her own feelings and needs. By giving her room to be "displeasing," a girl or woman can freely express *anger*. Which can present itself as annoyance, frustration, hurt, resentment, disappointment, and so many other TOTALLY NORMAL HUMAN EMOTIONS.

It's wildly stressful trying to be perfect and likable. Humans aren't built for that kind of pressure, and without an outlet for those unpleasant feelings it will eventually cause an explosion.

So now, when I'm addressing worries about being "displeasing" or "unlikable" with teenage girls, I ask some questions:

"So what if they don't like you?"

"What if they disapprove?"

"What if you disappoint them?"

"What if you tell them no?"

Instead of running and hiding from these questions (and the uncomfortable feelings they cause), we sit with them instead. I create space for her to vent, and after a lot of consideration and discussion, the wisdom that flows from teenage girls' brains has been revelatory for me.

Fifteen-year-old Keisha told me, "I have to do what's right for me, because that's all I can do. It's the only thing in my control."

Fourteen-year-old Charlee said, "They disapprove of me because we have different values. I'm not going to change my values for them."

Fifteen-year-old Lucia reflected, "I guess part of life is disappointing people sometimes. I can't make everyone happy."

Sixteen-year-old Zandy said, "It'll be hard to tell them no, but that feels better than saying yes, because that's not my truth."

All of these responses are incredibly powerful. They're honoring a girl's needs, values, and truth, and they are actively choosing themselves over other people—other people they can't control anyway. They're not letting someone have power over their choices, but instead, they're connecting to their own heart and making choices that feel right to them.

Their responses remind me of a quote from author Tarryn Fisher that I love: "Let people feel the weight of who you really are, and let them fucking deal with it."

Other people's reactions are not our responsibility. Plus, people are perceiving us through their own lens. I've found that when someone is judging me, it's usually because they're harshly judging themselves in the very same way. Their judgment comes from their own wounds and baggage, and it has very little to do with me.

That said, risking disapproval and judgment can definitely feel scary. What if I vulnerably share my true self, and they don't like that version of me? Yeah, that hurts. But bending and twisting myself into some fake person that I'm guessing people will like? That's a shittier option. There's a good chance people won't like that phony person either, and then I have nothing. At least with the first option, I can be myself.

Witnessing the people-pleasing struggle that teenage girls endure has been a vivid mirror for me. I've found that in reducing my inau-thentic people-pleasing, I've also weeded out some really draining people from my life. I used to have a lot of energy vampires around me who would profit off my never-ending well of giving (all in an attempt to make them like me). When I started having healthy boundaries, those vampires weren't happy. They revealed themselves quickly, and after a lot of self-work in this department, I was finally like, "Nope. I'm done."

I had to actively choose not to give them power over me anymore. And thankfully, this opened up so much new energy for the type of people in my life who like me for exactly who I am. I started to attract more of these types of people, and now when I choose to make people around me happy, I do it out of a wholeness and peace that isn't attached to their approval.

The truth is, people like authentic people who are connected to their feelings and their true nature, who are comfortable with themselves. Authenticity is a vibration that attracts other happy, authentic people. Those who want you to be happy without wanting to change you. These are the kinds of people who don't put their needs above yours and expect you to be pleasing at all times.

Freeing ourselves from people-pleasing is a journey of authenticity. It's a liberating choice that's letting me be me, letting you be you, letting teenage girls be who they want to be, and letting everyone be human.

Society has tried to convince girls that people-pleasing is good for them, and that making everyone else happy will make her happy, but it won't. We need to teach a girl that who should come first should be herself. —HAZEL, AGE 17

✦ "It's fine" tells the world not to worry about you, which is an unhealthy state that puts other people's needs before your own.

✦ The drive to be likable creates disconnection from your authentic self because it's twisting your identity to match someone else's expectations.

✦ It's impossible to control whether someone likes you. The only person who you truly have the power to make happy is yourself.

✦ People's judgments reflect their own insecurities, which is not your problem.

✦ Holding space to process displeasing feelings like anger can help someone healthily connect to their authentic self rather than living behind a mask of people-pleasing.

CHAPTER SIX

# COMPLIMENTS

*One kind word can warm three winter months.*
—Japanese proverb

A lot of people saw this chapter title and were like, "What? This feels a little basic." Yeah, I hear you. But you should also know that this chapter has the potential to positively and radically change your entire dynamic with not only your daughter, if you have one, but also with everyone in your life.

I know that no one is against giving compliments, but I've learned from teenage girls that we could be doing so much better, approaching the situation very differently.

If you observe women interact, at all ages, you'll notice they compliment each other a lot. It usually has to do with looks—I like your hair, outfit, jewelry, purse, shoes, etc. These types of compliments have become a reflex among women that I would classify as a social formality to indicate that you're . . . nice.

We've become so accustomed to this type of complimenting that it feels weird when a woman doesn't respond by complimenting you back, usually about the same external thing: your hair, outfit, jewelry, purse, shoes, etc. Now, maybe you like these types of compliments, which is okay, but I would love to challenge the larger dynamic and push for something more fulfilling.

The same people-pleasing drive exists in that dynamic, which leads us down a self-focused path. When I'm wanting someone to like me, I compliment them in order to make them like me (it doesn't feel good to admit that). In that situation, I'm using a compliment to manipulate someone's feelings about me. Making it about me.

Teenage girls have walked me through the reasons why they don't feel like they're getting complimented. I'll be specifying their experiences in this chapter, but I can't reinforce enough that the lessons they share are for *everyone*. The space I want to explore focuses on accessing an openhearted generosity that truly sees and celebrates another person. It will generate feelings inside of you that are far more fulfilling and uplifting than a manipulative "please like me" compliment that will leave you feeling needy and lacking.

People will pick up on a needy vibe, and it most likely won't earn you any friends. I feel fortunate to say that I've always been a very social person who can make friends pretty easily. It's not some magical talent I've had since birth. It's a practice in how I choose to show up for people. When people acknowledge my social skills, they usually ask, "What's the trick?"

If I'm going to give a quick, straightforward, starting-place answer to that, I respond with:

*"Assume that absolutely everyone is feeling insecure."*

Now I'm not usually a fan of assumptions, but I've come to learn that it's a pretty safe bet to assume everyone is feeling insecure. Not feeling "enough" is one of those stone-cold facts of being human that has driven us toward the greatest innovations but also birthed the boldest tyrants.

When I assume that someone is insecure, I find myself forgetting about my own insecurities, and instead, I approach the person with more compassion and authenticity. This approach has opened doors for me in unimaginable ways, and interestingly, I've spent a lot of quality time with famous, powerful, and prestigious people, who I promise are all very insecure like the rest of us. I bring all this up because I've found that acknowledging our universal insecurity is the starting point to understanding kindness and compassion.

In working with teenage girls, I swim in a vast sea of insecurity every single day as I help them navigate through their anxieties. You can physically see insecurity hijacking a teenage girl's spine through her hunched posture and slumped shoulders. I trace a lot of this insecurity to others squashing her bright shining spirit, but for now, I will accept this reality as is and address what I've learned from engaging with this vulnerable space.

Aisha is a 17-year-old living in a chaotic household with parents who are very absorbed in their own lives and who have little time for not only Aisha but also her ten-year-old sister, Nia. Aisha spends a lot of her time taking care of Nia, trying to give her the love and attention she longs for. Aisha also stays diligently on top of her advanced classes and recently received a full-ride college scholarship. From the outside, adults really only see that Aisha is "successfully" juggling her life, and are quick to compliment her straight As. They think that in order for her to be accomplishing so much, then she must be feeling confident, not insecure. They might give her a quick compliment of "You're so kind," or "You're so responsible!" but it never goes much further than that.

With the rapacious insecurity that is consuming the air a teenage girl is trying to breathe, I've learned that a girl needs so much more than that. During our weekly FaceTime, Aisha told me about her struggles with Nia fighting too much with kids at school (something that shouldn't be her problem). I took a beat, looking at her with all the love in the world.

"Aisha, you are doing an amazing job caring for your sister and helping her find her way. I know you want her to be the best she can be, and with a sister like you, she'll have a model in her life of someone who loves people generously and who makes responsible choices. I'm in awe of how you juggle your responsibilities with school, volunteering, extracurriculars, and caring for your sister. It's an inspiration the way you manage your time and commit your whole heart to anything you do. I know that you deal with so much anxiety and stress, which is completely valid, and at the same time, you care deeply and abundantly for your friends. I want to acknowledge how much goodness you give to the world and say that you deserve all of that same goodness in return."

Aisha started to cry, and through the flood of her emotion, she whispered, "Thank you. No one ever says stuff like that to me."

Adults never say things like that to her? Not only is that distressing, but it's also such a missed opportunity. I believe that people might be thinking these things about another person, but for some reason, they guard and withhold super-meaningful compliments. People can handle giving quick, surface-oriented compliments, but insightful and detailed compliments? That's the territory we need to explore. The lesson that I've deeply learned in working with teenage girls:

*Say the compliments you're thinking, out loud. State your appreciation frequently and thoroughly, even if it seems obvious. Specifically compliment the values, actions, and character traits that help a person feel seen, really seen.*

Why *don't* we say these types of compliments out loud? Teenage girls have a lot of wise thoughts on this. First up, 16-year-old Peeta told me, "People aren't complimenting each other because they think the other person already knows that about themselves. They think maybe someone has already told them or maybe they hear it a lot. But in reality, people are rarely complimenting each other in a big way."

I agree, because unfortunately, I often think to myself, *This woman is so amazing, she must already know all the ways she's amazing*, and then I don't say anything. Behavioral science studies conducted by three researchers from Stanford, Cornell, and the Wharton School further expanded this idea when they "consistently found that people underestimated how good their compliment would make the recipient feel. Compliment-givers tend to believe the other person won't enjoy their interaction as much as they actually do; in fact, they often believe that their exchange will probably make the person a little uncomfortable. Yet, consistently, receiving a compliment brightens people's day much more than anticipated, leaving them feeling better, and less uncomfortable, than givers expect."[1]

This research is not talking about complimenting someone's appearance and body, which indeed can cause some discomfort that

I'll cover later in the chapter Beauty. Instead, we're talking about discomfort around sharing something positive about people's personalities, individuality, and character. Sadly, I just think people aren't used to doing it. Complimenting someone's hair is a lot easier than looking deeper into a person's character.

In asking teenage girls for their wisdom on this issue, one of the uncomfortable excuses girls have highlighted for why people avoid giving heartfelt affirmation is because people want their compliments to "really matter." If they're given in excess, then it "weakens" them. When girls tell me this, they're often struggling because they don't agree with it, but they're wondering if I think it's true. I tell them:

"That's bullshit."

I've found that this mentality often develops in a childhood environment where parents rarely give compliments, and in order to cope, the brain has had to make sense of it with limiting ideas like this. I've found, in a profound way, that as long as a compliment is grounded in sincerity, there is a never-ending abundance of love, care, and appreciation that people can both give and receive.

If anything, I've witnessed that the more it happens, the more the characteristic that's being complimented grows *stronger* for teenage girls (not weaker). It'll blossom and expand in inspiring directions. Overall, I believe that whatever you give energy to grows bigger. And it's a choice. You can choose to give loving compliments abundantly, or you can hold them back.

In that same realm of thought, teenage girls brought up a topic again and again when I asked them about multiple chapters in this book. They told me that starting at a young age, they feel like their parents didn't affirm them, because they wanted to make sure that they didn't get cocky. Fourteen-year-old Juliette sums up a lot of the girls' thoughts with:

"Parents feel like it's their duty to keep girls grounded, because NO ONE likes a bossy girl. They're worried we'll get an ego. We're supposed to be humble, giving, and polite at all times."

At a younger age, confidence can often look like bossiness, and yes, society harshly bulldozes that situation, leaving scars that I know well. How we socialize a girl into self-doubt and restrict her self-expression will be explored in future chapters, but girls are not wrong, and this situation continues into adulthood. Eighteen-year-old Harper got particularly impassioned on this topic and didn't hold back:

"I think it's ridiculous how parents withhold compliments from a girl because they don't want her to get a big ego. Women having big egos, *that isn't a thing*. Society isn't fearing a woman's ego—it's fearing a woman's confidence. It's easier to make a woman who doesn't know her worth be subservient. A woman who knows her worth is what society is actually scared of."

Harper couldn't stop talking about this topic for our entire lunch because it struck such a nerve. I think this issue feeds into another situation where women and girls have a very hard time *receiving* compliments. At this point, I consider it a part of the societal performance of womanhood to brush away compliments with:

"Oh, this old thing, I got it on sale," or "I don't know about that, but I'm trying," or "It wasn't a big deal." Rather than just saying:

"Thank you."

At such a young age, just like Juliette pointed out, girls have been taught to be selfless and giving, which often leads to minimizing accomplishments, making it very uncomfortable to receive acknowledgment.

Sixteen-year-old Lori noted, "Compliments are hard to receive because they're hard to believe. In-depth compliments can be a shock, kind of confusing, or unexpected because they don't happen a lot. Which means, we should be giving those compliments more, so we can get better at receiving them."

I've also found that women are told to always be improving, to always be doing more to better themselves. This brings me to another biting excuse that I've heard repeatedly from teenage girls:

"Parents and teachers don't give meaningful compliments, because then, they think we won't try as hard, that we won't be motivated to work harder. Like we'll give up once we've gotten the compliment."

It's sad that this type of backward reasoning even exists. Did a *lack* of compliments actually motivate me to work harder as a teenager? I can see how someone would think that, but I think that all it truly did was make me feel shitty. Like nothing I could do was ever good enough.

It's upsetting that we don't know how to give compliments in a way that helps each other feel seen. It's a treasured and free gift that you can give to someone at any moment. But in order to do this, we need to listen deeply to the person, listening for something that feels unique to them. *Specificity* makes the acknowledgment come alive. It's the difference between someone saying, "You're so responsible," versus "How you manage to remember every single thing you need, several days in advance, as you bounce between your divorced parents' houses, is extraordinary. You rarely forget an item because you're a badass who strategically thinks of *everything*. I would say you're a really responsible teenager, because most adults couldn't manage what you manage."

Hearing that type of compliment as I was growing up would have no doubt helped me feel seen and understood, and it feels healing to write it now. Maybe we all should be writing out the compliments that our inner teenager wished for during those years that we struggled. Delivering and receiving these kinds of compliments today can heal our triggers and create room for more generosity with the teenage girls in our life.

Particularly, acknowledging specificity, uniqueness, even someone's "weirdness," is where people light up. If someone calls me "friendly," I'm like, okay, thanks. "Friendly" has many different looks. My version tends to be pretty high energy. If someone called me an "openhearted force of positive energy who lights up people's lives," then I would feel so deeply celebrated. I would want to give more energy to that part of myself. I would step into that part of my identity with more love, creating a genuine, healthy confidence—not ego.

This brings me to the next uncomfortable excuse that I've uncovered alongside teenage girls. Maybe we don't say anything because we're too focused on ourselves? We're wishing someone would compliment us?

That sounds like something our flawed humanness would be doing, so it's important to address it more thoroughly.

I think of genuine compliments as a flow of energy that's like undulating sound waves. Like the sound a cricket makes in a forest of animals. The sound of its chirping ripples in all directions. If you're not creating your own sound waves then there is no energy flow around you at all. It's quiet. But you can always be the first source of the sound wave, chirping until the sounds of the forest respond and reverberate around you. Chirping your way into generosity and abundance.

This means: Start giving wholehearted compliments, and you'll start receiving a lot more in return.

And not only do these types of compliments spread good energy, they also make the person giving the compliment more likable. In addition to my first relational trick, "Assume that everyone is insecure," I also have this one:

*People will like you when they like how they see themselves through your eyes.*

If you can see the unique, best version of someone, and then affirm it with words, people will automatically be drawn to that energy. I know a lot of parents who deeply wish for their teenage daughter to like them more. I'm telling you, this is it. I'm giving you a pathway in. A teenage girl likes someone who genuinely holds her in high regard and verbalizes it with specificity, because it helps her like herself. People, including teenage girls, want to be around someone who sees and brings out their best self.

To be clear again, I'm not talking about a people-pleasing manipulation to make someone like you, and I'm not talking about bullshitting and sucking up. You might also feel like you already give your daughter lots of compliments, and she's still not liking you. In that case, I usually recommend increasing the length or specificity of the compliment, but it's also incredibly helpful if the person giving the compliment is filled with *genuine enthusiasm.*

I want to expand the conversation around enthusiasm because it shines brightly within the wisdom of teenage girls. They deeply understand the power of an exclamation point. Enthusiasm may not come naturally to you, but I would encourage you to explore and push your boundaries with it. People thrive when they receive enthusiasm, and I believe it's an underestimated spiritual gift. I recently learned that the etymology of the word *enthusiasm* is the Greek word *enthousiasmos*, which means "divine inspiration" or "having God within." It's sourced deeper in the soul than positivity. I find that people absorb the vibration of someone's enthusiasm in a way that is healing and empowering.

I'm not talking about a forced, over-the-top enthusiasm. In order for a person to express *genuine* enthusiasm, they need to be connected to their own heart. I believe that when enthusiasm is sincerely given, there's an abundantly loving energy that travels from one heart to the other. It's a type of compliment that doesn't use words, and it's contagious.

Another way to experience the deeper connection that results from compliments is to give enthusiasm to things that a teenage girl likes. I'm talking about things she's interested in, that might seem small to you, but are big to her. That is where so much magic happens. When I reached out to 16-year-old Zandy for her thoughts on this matter, she texted:

"Society hates everything teenage girls like. If teenage girls like it, then it's considered stupid, silly, unserious. So what if I like *Twilight*?!! Maybe try caring about something I like!"

Whether it's a movie, TV show, fashion blog, or an activity she's doing that afternoon, expressing enthusiastic, genuine interest in what she cares about will make her feel good, and it will feel like you're complimenting her identity.

It's definitely an exclamation point situation. The language might feel a bit exaggerated, but if you can reach into your heart and find your honest, authentic expression of enthusiasm, it can go such a long way in creating a loving, positive environment for not only a teenage girl *but everyone in your life.*

With the girls I work with, we fill our process with so much enthusiasm and affirmation. Whatever we focus our thoughts and energy on grows bigger. I work to empower the good, and consequently, our time is filled with so much laughter and fun. I can't count the number of times parents have told me how utterly shocked they are to hear that their kid is laughing while doing math. They act like it's some type of sorcery. That feels accurate for me, because there is indeed a magic and enchantment to a learning environment that's full of enthusiasm, compliments, empathy, and the chance to be seen as your full self. It's the bountiful breeding ground for self-confidence and empowerment. The girl is liking herself more because she likes how she's experiencing herself through my eyes, which are focused on her *brilliance.*

In contrast, I've never seen a teenage girl *critiqued* into more self-confidence. If you want a teenage girl to like you, not only could you increase the specificity, length, frequency, and enthusiasm of your compliments, you could also decrease (and maybe eliminate?) the amount of time spent critiquing her. I've found that a mom sometimes unconsciously picks apart her daughter because she herself endured it from her mom, and it's hard to break a pattern when there's no awareness around it.

This is also an area where girls feel like their parents' "don't get cocky" attitude comes in. You might compliment a girl a lot, but if you're also critiquing her a lot, then the criticism will undoubtedly be louder and more memorable for her.

Eighteen-year-old Celeste told me, "Critiques are often masked as something else, especially with girls. It's a mask like 'I'm protecting you and making sure you don't get hurt,' but it actually underestimates or even degrades us. It knocks down our self-esteem where we don't want to try anymore."

A sneaky way that I see a critique show up is through "teaching" her. I often see adults stuck in a constant state of "teaching" a girl and looking to the next thing to improve, consequently blowing by any opportunity for affirmation. When we're stuck only looking toward the next goalpost, we miss all the positive steps of growth along the way.

With tutoring, I have definitely fumbled this and gotten stuck in teaching mode. I was thinking that I'm better preparing her for life by always pushing her toward the next way to "improve" because it will "protect" her. However, when I do this, what a teenage girl hears from me is:

The cool things that you have already accomplished aren't good enough.

Without taking moments for affirmation and enthusiastic celebration along the way, it will feel like a never-ending cycle of needing to be better. A teenage girl is going through some serious identity-forming, and it's a process that will be severely impacted if she's only hearing a constant critique.

In response to a regular state of being evaluated, I see teenage girls erect their emotional walls and place guards at the door that carry the weapons of teen fury. Being hostile and vicious can certainly feel a lot safer when no one seems to see or value your authentic self. Rather than building confidence, that rage does everything it can to protect the insecurity hiding behind the walls.

I've learned that in order to tear down those walls for both teenagers and adults alike, we need to intentionally change our style of complimenting. This takes slowing down and becoming present in the moment. My brain can be so busy thinking of the next thing I want to say or worried about what people think of me, that I'm not seeing the extraordinary teenage girl that sits in front of me. When that happens, I'm not present enough to deeply listen. However, when I listen to her with presence and the intention of seeing her full self, it often becomes clear what type of compliment could light up her day.

If a compliment enters your mind in moments like that, choose to say it *out loud*. I promise that the other person needs to hear it. At any given moment, each of us has a gift inside of us to give to someone else. Choose to give that gift. It might feel like you're stating the obvious, and even if you are, that human being standing in front of you needs to hear it.

In an ideal world, would we all get our confidence from intrinsic self-love? Of course, but in reality, we're living in a world of interconnectedness, dealing with our insecurities, because we're imperfect human beings. People. Need. Each. Other.

I've learned through teenage girls that we underestimate how much we see ourselves through other people's eyes. If we're going to grow beyond what we know right now, we're going to need to see ourselves through eyes that cherish and empower us. And if this is all a bit cheesy for you, I ask that you simply try it.

This week, compliment five people in your life, using more than two sentences to do so. You can say it in person, via email, text, or whatever you want, just try it. Push the excuses and discomfort to the side, because when you see the person's heart fill with gratitude, and you see them smile with a bit more self-love, you'll feel really good too. It's the type of feeling good that brings peace and wholeness. There is a ripple effect of kindness that flows out of intentional compliments, and I've learned that everyone, absolutely everyone, is needing that generosity right now.

## Compliments mean a lot more than someone might show. —OLIVIA, AGE 15

---

✦ Say the compliment you're thinking, out loud, right now, because absolutely everyone is feeling insecure and could use the genuine encouragement.

✦ Instead of critiquing others, increase the frequency, specificity, and length of sincere compliments that you give to others in order to create a more empowering and loving environment around you.

✦ Genuine enthusiasm is a contagious gift that creates heartfelt connections with others.

✦ It's important to reflect on how and why women, in particular, have been socialized to have a hard time receiving compliments.

✦ Complimenting values, actions, and character traits that are unique to an individual helps someone feel seen and understood.

## CHAPTER SEVEN

# RADICAL HONESTY

*And at last you'll know with surpassing certainty that only
one thing is more frightening than speaking your truth.
And that is not speaking.*[1]
—Audre Lorde

Yeah, you're right. You're never going to use this math that I'm teaching you."

I say this a lot to teenage girls. Math is the number one subject that I tutor because every student usually wants help with it. We spend hours upon hours, years upon years, together learning math and studying for math tests. I earn income from teaching math, so one might think I'd justify the time and effort. I'm working with girls who are usually struggling in the subject and who have zero interest in pursuing STEM careers. So, when I'm asked by a student (and I'm undoubtedly always asked), "Am I ever going to use this math in my life?" I'm honest. Factoring a polynomial? Finding the derivative? Proving two triangles are congruent?

"Nope. You're definitely not."

Sometimes, I get into a bit more detail about how they might use it on a standardized test or in a gen ed course in college, stuff that technically means they're "using it," but by no means do I see ninth through twelfth grade math curriculum show up in an average adult's daily life. Unfortunately, we're rarely teaching any type of financial math in schools, and kids are usually only taking precalculus because colleges like to see it on their transcript. My frustrations with this situation aside, I refuse to lie to girls about it.

When I answer a question like this with such blunt honesty, the girl's face usually erupts into a smile and she looks at me wide-eyed. Teenage girls LOVE radical honesty. When I mentioned to Addison, who is now 24, that I was writing this chapter, she exclaimed:

"Oh my gosh, Chelsey, do you remember when I was twelve and I grabbed your phone and saw that reminder for *Pill* on there? I asked you what it was for, and you told me it was for your birth control? I couldn't believe you told me the truth!!! I thought for sure you were going to lie to me about some antibiotic!"

It's been 12 years since that happened, and *she still remembers it.* That's how impactful the truth is to teenage girls.

Addison went on to point out, "And it was so important because that was the first time I learned about how you have to take the birth control pill at the same time every day. My school didn't teach me that. You being honest with me opened up such a positive and educational conversation. And it made me trust you!"

When I respond truthfully to hard-hitting questions from girls, I open the exciting floodgates of honesty. She starts sharing openly too. A confluence of truth instantaneously creates *trust.* Permissioning this space of radical honesty not only creates trust between us, it also generates a trust within her sense of self and personal power.

Consequently, the lesson I've learned from teenage girls' wise affinity for truth-telling is that *we all have a deep need for radical honesty because it's the space where authentic connections thrive and revolutionary change begins.*

Teenage girls love radical honesty because they feel like everyone around them is constantly lying to them. I don't think they're exaggerating. When I asked girls for their thoughts on this topic, they unanimously agreed that adults aren't truthful with them.

Sixteen-year-old Lori told me, "Adults try to cover the truth because they think we can't handle it. But we already know a lot more than they think, and it's not helping, it's hurting. It's like when someone whispers a secret to someone else right in front of you, and it makes you feel really uncomfortable."

As 17-year-old Madelyn says, "Adults think we're this subordinate group that can't comprehend complex issues, so they lie instead, underestimating our ability to engage critical thinking skills."

This statement might cause many adults to push back and exclaim, "Teenagers are the ones doing the lying!"

There is indeed a type of lying that shows very normal developmental stages for adolescents who are asserting their independence from their parents. However, I also believe they are reflecting the world around them.

Fifteen-year-old Marli sighed with frustration when she told me, "When parents blame and shame us for our mistakes, then yes, we'll start lying to avoid that type of punishment. But I'd much rather feel safe to tell the truth."

Sixteen-year-old Zandy agrees and takes it one step further. "Yes, kids lie, out of fear of consequences. But if parents just listened instead and tried to understand us rather than going straight to consequences, we wouldn't lie as much. I also lie because society makes me feel like it's not safe to be myself."

It feels pretty obvious to me that the world around us is doing a lot of lying. They aren't always huge lies, but subtler methods like hypocrisy, half-truths, omissions, and an overall lack of transparency establish a strong message. Not only will girls unconsciously model that behavior, but I find that teenage girls are *encouraged* to lie. It's part of the perfection and people-pleasing that society jams down her throat from a young age. Look perfect, act perfect, think perfectly, speak perfectly—all of which is impossible, so we're basically encouraging her to live a lie.

This performative state of being does not require huge lies. There are many small, daily habits that create a facade. If we actually shared our truth that life is hard, and we're all struggling, then we'd have to admit that we're not perfect and not always pleasing. That vulnerability would force us to really connect with the human being in front of us. Which is what teenage girls are starving for.

People, completely and utterly, underestimate a teenage girl's ability to detect bullshit, and she's *so over the bullshit*. I find that it often fuels her fury, as I've heard so many girls scream at their parents:

"Don't lie to me!!"

Teenage girls can acutely see through the show people put on to look good. It's why their insults are so cutting and accurate. She can see what you're trying to hide. It's not a safe environment to tell the truth if the adults around you aren't doing the same, so of course she puts up walls.

When someone chooses to be real with her, it's incredibly freeing and even thrilling. I add the word *radical* in front of *honesty* because the level of truth needs to feel almost dangerous. A level that sparks, *You have the courage to say that?*

Some of the topics that I've had the courage to talk to them about include the alcoholism in my family, my struggles with disordered eating, the devastation of a friend's suicide, and embarrassing career failures. I often see their shoulders relax with relief when I share these struggles because they stop feeling so alone in the world's pain. I've had a lot of girls tell me some of their really distressing struggles surrounding abuse, heartbreak, sexual assault, bullying, and usually after recounting the horror, they immediately say that good ole phrase I've already spent time in these pages dissecting:

"But it's fine. I'm fine."

And again, instead of assuring them that everything will be better soon (which I truthfully can't know with certainty), I offer them the truth that I do know:

"It's not fine. It's awful that any of that happened to you. I can hold space for your pain, anger, and sadness around this if you want to share it with me. You don't need to manage my feelings, assuring me that you're okay. It's okay to not be okay. We can acknowledge truthfully the fucking awfulness that you went through, if you want."

I'm recounting this type of exchange again because it's so critically important. Before, I noted how a girl was people-pleasing by diminishing her needs in a moment like this, but now I want to take it a step further and sink my teeth into the fact that "fine" is *not the truth.*

When I respond with the truth—"It's not fine"—then a girl usually starts crying and courageously tells me many more details that she's stored deep inside because she felt like no adult could handle listening to it all. She felt like no one could handle her truth.

Usually, adults are intensely monitoring their own comfort levels with people's honesty because it can spark a lot of fear. A teenage girl's level of honesty is certainly hard-hitting, so I see parents choose to put up emotional walls and try to control or manipulate the situation out of fear rather than simply listening.

I've learned that all this fear is so unnecessary. I've witnessed worse consequences appear in response to subtle lies than any response to the truth. However, I've had to be intentional about creating a safe space. I invite the truth, request the truth, and even push for the truth, and I make sure to tell her:

"There are no consequences here for you telling the truth. I'm only here to listen. We can process if you want, but saying the truth out loud is healing in itself."

If a girl is prone to people-pleasing, then it's also really important that I emphasize how her truth will not affect how much I like her. A very liberating moment often follows when she starts really telling me her honest thoughts on things. Those thoughts cut deep, and I'm here for it. I usually respond with simple, sincere acknowledgment:

"So true." "That sucks." "You're right."

This builds trust, and over time, we create more and more moments like this that feel so liberating because they're safe. We're not letting fear dictate what we share.

Parents are often worried about discussing serious topics like drugs and alcohol. There are no definitive answers on the best approach, but I have found that an environment where it feels safe to say the radical truth, starting at an early age, opens up more options. I always try to model the behavior that I want to inspire in a girl while still being honest about my personal growth along the way. A teenage girl will often match my level of honesty, so if I'm showing her that I feel safe to be honest with her, it will inspire that same sense of safety from her. I do this without any agenda or secret lesson that I want to teach her because that's when walls go up.

And it doesn't always have to be serious topics. So often people tell little lies in order to manipulate someone's behavior in a way they think is helpful. Parents have shared their worries with me that if I tell a girl she won't ever use precalculus in her adult life, then it'll somehow make her unmotivated, or she'll give up on the class, affecting her transcripts for college. I tell them that I've seen the opposite reaction occur when a girl hears my radical honesty (that she's definitely not using precalc as an adult). I watch girls become more motivated because they finally know what's going on and how to play the game. Their ability in math is no longer attached to their self-worth.

Before, there was so much anxiety linked to math because they thought if they failed at it, then they'd fail at life. When they learn that's not true, they feel liberated and often find it much easier to get the work done without the extra mental stress. I find that the little lies, like "She must be good at quadratic equations," is what keeps her spiraling on an axis that feels unstable—*because it's not the truth.* Seriously, we all know that you can succeed in life without understanding this:

$$x = \frac{-b \pm \sqrt{b^2 - 4ac}}{2a}$$

And after I tell her that, she's usually earning an A in math within the month. She just needed to hear the truth, so she could make the choices that feel good for her. Again, we're back to that idea of "choice."

Teenage girls will make wise and healthy choices if they're given truthful information. This is also why I think it's a loving act to tell someone the truth. It's an act of respect and trust. It creates the authenticity that everyone is craving. Within that space, it's also important to let a girl find her truth. I can be real with her, without forcing something onto her.

Fourteen-year-old Tisha had gotten into an argument with a friend at school on how they were going to accept new members into their environmental club. Tisha wanted it to be difficult to get in, and her friend wanted to include everyone. Tisha was clearly still upset with the situation because she was stuck on being right in the argument. I asked her if she wanted to talk it out, and she agreed. I dove in, phrasing everything as a question, working toward getting closer to her truth. It can take some more "Why?"s to lead into a conversation like this, but I'm always a fan of being straightforward.

"Why did you start the club? Let's get to the truth of that."

"To save the planet, because otherwise we're doomed." I smile at her dramatic tone.

"That's a good idea. So can I be straight with you?"

When I'm entering a radical honesty space, I like to frame it with a question that invites her consent. As soon as I say it, she jumps in. "I know what you're going to say."

"Oh yeah, cool, what?"

"Having more members in the club will help save the planet more."

"Does that seem true to you?"

She begrudgingly looks at me and utters, "Yeah . . ."

I see her resistance, so I greet it with warmth and respect.

"Hey, you have nothing to prove to me and I think you're amazing no matter what. I'm asking questions because I respect you, which means I'm going to keep it real." It's so important to create emotional safety and respect when she's questioning and trying to find her truth.

She says, "I just wanted the club to have an exclusive, cool feeling to it."

"I get it. Is that in sync with the mission of the club?"

She looks at me knowingly. I love to pair honesty with humor, so I smile at Tisha with some lighthearted sarcasm.

"I don't know, maybe the environment does indeed only want cool people supporting it, and it's like, 'Please don't let losers recycle!' "

She starts laughing, and I playfully continue, "Maybe being cool *is* the solution to saving the environment." We laugh together, relaxing into how calling out the truth in a silly way can positively shift the tone of a difficult conversation. With warmth I say, "Or is recycling what makes someone cool? I'm confused now, so tell me how you want to handle this." I make sure to always show her respect and put the choice in her court.

"I'm wrong. . . . I just got so attached to my idea."

"That's okay, I do that too." Tisha smiles, not feeling alone. I make sure to fill the space with a compliment: "I think it's really cool that your opinion can adapt. It's a really mature quality to be able to think about things from different perspectives. It shows how smart you are."

She smiles proudly, and I kid you not, she said, "Thanks. I don't usually admit when I'm wrong, but it felt safe to say the truth with you."

I find that girls are so often bracing for impact, ready to be criticized, that they're living in a state of tension as a defense mechanism. A safe environment for the truth, one filled with levity and respect, can set them free.

Honesty around mess-ups and imperfections is refreshing and liberating because we're all human beings, and we mess up. When I'm radically honest about my mistakes and shortcomings, teenage girls open up to me. Radical honesty is the path to something that feels authentic. If you try to appear like everything is going perfectly, deep down, people will know you're lying.

Additionally, if we can fill that space with the type of compliments that help people feel truly seen and understood, then it's game changing. Deeper connections and healing flow in.

That said, it can be hard to be radically honest with others if you're not being radically honest with yourself. For me, it's been a muscle that has gotten stronger and stronger with more practice. It's a practice that involves listening to my heart and gut rather than the noise of my mind that wants to believe "perfection" is the safer bet.

I think we're scared of the type of power that flows from the truth. It has the ability to disrupt entrenched patterns and provoke self-reflection. Radical honesty cuts into someone's core and urges them to question things. There are a lot of systems in this world that could use some major *questioning*. Powerful systems have maintained their status because there aren't enough people boldly speaking the truth and acting on what they think is right.

Eighteen-year-old Harper passionately elaborates on this idea: "Speaking truth to power means calling out human suffering even when it makes other people uncomfortable. People are so used to the broken systems that we live under that the truth is going to be uncomfortable, but that's why it's so important."

The phrase that Harper used, "speaking truth to power," was popularized during the civil rights movement. It was first said by Bayard Rustin, a Black Quaker who advocated for nonviolent methods to fight against social injustice.[2] The meaning behind the words encourages someone to challenge those people and systems in power by calling out the truth about the injustices they're responsible for and by demanding change. Those in power usually prefer the status quo because that's how they got the power in the first place.

Historically, speaking truth has been an impetus for change, and I think it's one of teenage girls' most powerful weapons against injustice.

Considering teenage girls' love for honesty, I find that it also makes them more fearless when it comes to speaking truth to power. At 15 years old, in Pakistan, Malala Yousafzai was consistently speaking the truth, challenging the Taliban's unjust laws that deny girls an education. Her truth was such a threat to their regime that they shot her. Thankfully, she survived and won the Nobel Peace Prize two years later. A teenage girl's honest voice was so powerful that it threatened one of the world's most dangerous militant organizations and was awarded the world's most prestigious prize in creating peaceful change.

Malala's stakes were very high, but feminist scholar and activist Audre Lorde provides a critical reflection for women not facing life-threatening reactions, but who are still choosing to stay silent with their truth. She asks:

" 'What's the worst that could happen to me if I tell this truth?' Unlike women in other countries, our breaking silence is unlikely to have us jailed, 'disappeared' or run off the road at night. Our speaking out will irritate some people, get us called bitchy or hypersensitive and disrupt some dinner parties. And then our speaking out will permit other women to speak, until laws are changed and lives are saved and the world is altered forever."[3]

Teenage girls deeply understand this. They love their weapon of truth, and with some direction and encouragement, they can learn how to positively direct its force. Seventeen-year-old Kat, whose smile normally lights up a room, was not smiling when she learned that she was going to have to wear a white dress at her high school graduation. The tradition made the girls look like they were in wedding dresses, and felt antiquated and like a nod to purity culture. Kat started sharing her truth at school: "I wanted to feel like a scholar in a cap and gown at my graduation, not like I'm marrying my school or telling the world I'm now available for marriage." Historically, that used to be a thing, and girls her age would debut in society in a white dress, announcing they were available for marriage. Kat was like, "Oh hell no."

Kat rallied the support of her classmates, giving permission to other girls to share their truth about the situation. Turns out, many girls felt the same way. Inspired and motivated, Kat took her truth to the administration. The powers in charge were jolted and hesitant because they were caught up in the tradition of how they'd always done it. The truth makes people uncomfortable because then it means they might need to change. Change causes a lot of discomfort.

That said, Kat made it happen. She spoke out eloquently with the truth and generated lasting change. Girls at that school no longer have to wear white dresses at graduation.

I've found that adults can be so entrenched in what they know to be normal that they've lost sight of what needs to change. Questioning power and systems takes courage, and as scholar and historian Howard Zinn, renowned for his truth-telling accounts of American history, expresses:

"But I suppose the most revolutionary act one can engage in is . . . to tell the truth."[4]

Teenage girls have a revolutionary power inside them. It starts with radical truth. They haven't lost sight of what's important and authentic. When a girl speaks the truth out loud, she feels free to be her authentic self, which creates trust with others and within herself. That courageous honesty can create both healing and powerful change.

It's powerful to truthfully say what's on your mind, because it seems like no one is doing it. —JADE, AGE 15

---

+ Radical honesty not only creates trust within relationships, it also creates trust within your own sense of self.

+ It's hard to be honest with others if you're not being honest with yourself.

+ If someone isn't telling the truth, it's probably because they don't feel safe to share and are scared of being judged or shamed.

+ A performative state of being (focused on perfection and people-pleasing) is a state of lying to oneself and the world, and it's liberating and empowering to step into your truth.

+ Teenage girls' natural ability to speak truth to power is an underestimated force for progress.

CHAPTER EIGHT

# SELF-DOUBT

*You can either waltz boldly onto the stage of life and live the way*
*you know your spirit is nudging you to, or you can sit quietly*
*by the wall, receding into the shadows of fear and self-doubt.*
—Oprah Winfrey[1]

irl Power!!" "Girl PWR!!!" "Self-Confidence is the Best Outfit!"
"Girl Boss!" "Always Wear Your Invisible Crown!" "Boss Lady!!"
"Confidence is Beautiful!!!"

Yeah, I got it . . . I got the message!! I'm supposed to have confidence. These statements are slapped all over T-shirts, tote bags, notebooks, backpacks, pencils, mugs, water bottles, and anything else that might INSPIRE YOU. And as cynical as I might sound about all of this confidence-pushing, I'm also here for it. Confidence is indeed a great feeling, and I would love to inspire girls to feel it, but I've found that it's way more complicated than that. One might question how I could have an entire book about teenage girls without a chapter entitled "Confidence." Well, here is the chapter, with the blaring, uncomfortable, unsettling title of "Self-Doubt" instead. That's the reality that I confront every day.

There's no world where simply telling a girl to "Be confident!" is going to work. There is too much self-doubt to unravel, similar to untangling the knots of eight necklaces that somehow conjoined in your jewelry box in the most frustrating way possible. It takes patience, focus, care, and tiny fingers to loosen those necklace knots, which isn't that different from untangling self-doubt. It's the choices we make within the tiny moments that inform the overall self-doubt/self-confidence spectrum.

When I ask 17-year-old Hazel to give me the answer to a math problem, there's always a pause. She looks at me with her warm, sheepish grin and expectant, twinkling eyes, thinking maybe if she pauses long enough that I'll jump in with the answer. I ask her again, and begrudgingly she utters an answer with a tone that's filled with self-doubt, convinced she is wrong.

But then I proclaim, "You're right!" (Which is most often the case.)

"Wait, really?? No . . ."

"You got the right answer, Hazel!"

"I really shouldn't . . ." (I jump in to finish the sentence with her because I know exactly what she's going to say.)

"*Doubt myself.*" I smirk lovingly at Hazel, and she bursts into laughter.

She exclaims, "You're going to make me that T-shirt, right?"

"Yes. I can't wait to make you a T-shirt that says, '*I really shouldn't doubt myself.*' "

She laughs again. "I definitely need that shirt!"

After years of Hazel responding to her own correct answers with self-doubt, we have now decided to laugh about it. It's gotten to be ridiculous, not just with Hazel, but with so many girls I work with. They are constantly saying with seemingly never-ending surprise at their correct answers: "I really shouldn't doubt myself."

I didn't give them these words—they're self-generated. Definitely not as catchy as the QUEEN OF CONFIDENCE shirt you'll see on Etsy, but certainly more authentic.

While I don't think it's news to anyone that teenage girls struggle with insecurity, you might not have expected self-doubt to be a fantastic area in which to explore a teenage girl's wisdom and power. I've learned from them that *as agonizing as self-doubt can be . . . when we engage and examine it, self-doubt can push us to confront fear, activate courage, and ultimately find self-acceptance.*

The authors of *The Confidence Code* books, Katty Kay and Claire Shipman, found in their research that there's no difference between girls' and boys' confidence until age eight, and then shit gets crazy. Between ages eight and fourteen, a girl's confidence drops by 30 percent.[2] If I could insert a horror-stricken emoji face here, I would. When girls are at their lowest point, at age fourteen, boys' confidence remains 27 percent higher. They've also found that a whopping eight out of ten girls want to feel more confident in themselves. That means only two out of ten girls are living in a reality that says, "I feel good about myself." While that's a horrible statistic, I don't think any of us are that surprised.

Those are some big numbers we need to reckon with if we care about teenage girls' well-being, so it's time to step into this mess, together.

When I enter this territory with teenage girls, the first thing I ask them to do is fake it. Fake the confidence. Wait, what, you ask? Hear me out.

When a girl is working through a homework problem with me, she will usually finish the question and then immediately say, "Right?"

To keep things moving along, I often respond with a yes, and it turns into a rhythm where she gets used to me telling her she's right. It's a problem because she starts becoming dependent on that confirmation, and I'm basically robbing her of the opportunity of discomfort. *The Opportunity of Discomfort!* It's similar to the gray zone discussed in the chapter Perfection.

It's a void of uncertainty where things don't feel black and white. It's the space where self-doubt storms in, and with its gnarly, grippy fist, takes hold of your thoughts and viciously twists them into a story of self-defeating insecurity.

So now, instead of filling that void with my repetitive and empty affirmation, I've introduced a new approach. I ask her to play a game with me. When she finishes a question, I stay silent. Even if she feels unsure about the answer, she can't ask me if it's right. Rather, she's going to boldly fake some confidence. I invite her to really play it up, own it, and be cocky!

When she first starts doing this, it's suuuuper uncomfortable for her. That type of confidence feels foreign to her. However, slowly but surely, she begins to experience what self-confidence feels like in her brain and body. Maybe it's not based on her truth, but it's an energy space that she rarely gets to explore with reckless abandon. It's so fun to watch her embrace the game of it all as I urge her on with encouragement. Eventually, her posture starts morphing to match her new attitude, boldly proclaiming:

"Watch me slay this question." "Oh, I got this!" "Wait, who's getting all the answers right? Oh right, it's me." "I'm dominating this math." "I'm not sure if people are ready for how good I am at this."

We laugh and lean into the performance even more. If we're on FaceTime, sometimes I even take a screenshot of her, because it's so fun to see her strike a bold, confident pose. She's experimenting with the feeling of self-confidence filling the void of uncertainty rather than self-doubt, and laughter and play are easing the discomfort.

It's an interesting space to play in, because, as I mentioned in the chapter Compliments, girls are really scared of being thought of as arrogant. When I asked 15-year-old Jade why she feels like she struggles with self-doubt, she wisely shared:

"When you're a little girl, everyone is telling you not to be bossy or cocky, so you learn to be self-deprecating. And then you internalize it, and it sticks. Now, I have a lot of self-doubt. It's made me scared to share my accomplishments, and sometimes I know I'm smarter than the boys in my honors chem class, but I don't want to act like I am. But then it's frustrating, because I also wanna tell the world, 'Don't dull my sparkle.' "

Agreed, Jade, yes, I also wish I could *shout* to the world, "DON'T DULL MY SPARKLE."

Unfortunately, it happens, and we're going to explore it more in this chapter.

But why am I calling this space the Opportunity of Discomfort?

Because it's a space of growth. Just like the gray zone discussed earlier, learning occurs when we can't rely on the security and comfort that binary thinking seemingly provides. Self-doubt is a state of tension that invites questioning. It can totally overrun the brain with a destructive force, or it can be an invitation . . . to confront and deal with our deepest, darkest fears (you know, fun stuff!).

Discomfort can be framed as an opportunity, like a flare gun announcing that this is a topic worth exploring. I dive into discomfort all the time with teenage girls, but I thoroughly and honestly explain what's going on, so they are a consenting and active participant. When this space is treated with a ton of love and care, it can bring about the type of conversations that invite and ignite growth.

The first place we focus is the *voice inside our brain*.

Negative self-talk, as it's often called, is the dominant weapon of self-doubt. Different modalities of therapy have different ways of addressing it, and I hope everyone gets the chance to explore their options. Here, I'll be sharing a process that evolved out of many conversations with teenage girls.

I'm not saying you need to guide this exact process with the teenage girl in your life. I'm saying do this with your own brain. If you want to have a conversation with a teenage girl about self-doubt, it will be better to come from a place of:

"This is how I'm struggling with self-doubt, and this is what I'm doing that's been helping me."

Not: "You need to do this, or you *should* do this."

A good starting point for harder conversations is always speaking from your own personal struggle. You might see her struggling in a similar way, but that doesn't mean your solution is going to be her solution. That's why it's good to keep things phrased as a question, so she can find her own answers.

When I watch a teenage girl work through a math problem, I can tell when a negative self-talk voice is creating a tornado inside her brain. A tornado that I find to be very common among women. I've asked teenage girls what the voice is saying, and these are some of the things they've told me:

"You're dumb." "You'll never get this." "Why are you even trying?" "This is really bad." "You're such an idiot." "No one likes you." "You're going to fail." "You're fat." "Everyone is saying bad things about you." "You're ugly." "You're not good enough to do this." "You're a failure."

When I notice that this voice is taking over, I ask her to share with me the exact words. I tell her that we're going to bring awareness to the voice, but we're not going to judge, get mad at, or beat ourselves up for this voice. We're simply bringing the voice out of the dark recesses of her mind and into the light. In solidarity, I share what my negative self-talk voice sounds like too. I assure her that everyone struggles with a negative voice inside their head.

Then, here's the key moment. I ask, "Where does this voice come from? Whose voice is it?"

Only a few, rare times have I gotten unsure eyes looking back at me, asking, "Mine?" Instead, the most common response is:

"Society's voice."

I love that answer, and out of caution, I always emphasize, "Right. It's. Not. Your. Voice."

Sometimes, the voice feels so familiar that it's pretty hard to untangle it from her own true, inner voice. In keeping it real, some girls have responded that the negative voice is their parents'. That's when it's particularly hard to untangle. Teachers and bullies are often mentioned as well.

To start separating the negative self-talk voice from her own voice, we lean into the Opportunity of Discomfort. I ask her to identify exactly when she's heard that voice, so that we can really nail down the facts of where it's coming from and how *it's not her voice.*

As she slowly finds some separation from that mean voice, then it's time for her to start connecting to her real, inner voice. Sometimes in this type of work, I've seen people coach a girl's new self-talk voice to be *really* kind and loving a bit too quickly. It can feel really forced to immediately start saying in your brain, "You're amazing!" I've found that we'll naturally resist something that feels inauthentically new, so I like to straddle the bridge of reality.

This is where the practice of radical honesty is helpful. I like to build a foundation of trust where we've allowed the candid truth to safely exist in our conversations. I like to take their instinctive understanding of radical honesty and connect it to how their inner voice will also feel truthful when they hear it. It's usually a process-oriented voice rather than a dramatic shift in how she perceives her identity. It'll often sound like: "This is hard, that's okay." "Take your time, you can do this." "Just be yourself." "You learned this." "Take it step-by-step." "The beauty standards of society are not real." "Don't care what they think." "I'm not bad at this." "Trust yourself."

Just like the experiment of practicing bold confidence, they need to hear this inner voice out loud and feel the new energy it creates inside them. If she doesn't know the words yet, I offer options and we figure out what uniquely resonates for her. Thankfully, I've found that the more we do it, the more this voice becomes louder and stronger.

One of my favorites that I've heard is, "I'm human, I can make mistakes."

I practice saying that one to myself because it helps me combat my tendency to seek "perfection," and instead, helps me embrace and accept my flaws. Over breakfast, 18-year-old Davina tilts her head and reflects on the voice inside her mind. She frowns with frustration, making the same connection:

"This mean voice is tied to society's expectation for us to be perfect. We're beating ourselves up because we're told there's no reason to do something if it isn't going to be amazing."

Perfectionism and People-Pleasing are very old friends with Self-Doubt. It's like they started a club together in childhood and made a blood oath to work as a team to systematically annihilate the potential of women.

I'm trying to shut that club down, alongside teenage girls who are desperately aching for their own voices to be heard.

However, there's an incredibly powerful ringleader of this club who has an aggressive leadership style that's all-consuming, sneaky, and vicious. This leader's name is FEAR and it can be a real asshole.

Teenage girls are not fooled. They know Fear is the leader of this violent gang.

In my discussion with Davina, she further elaborated that, "Society hammers into women that they should be fearful of everything. Taught to be uncomfortable and scared all the time. It's like we're never supposed to feel safe."

This is why I like to lean into this conversation so much with a teenage girl, because if I can unhook the grip that fear has on her life, then so much power is unlocked. A point that Davina nailed when she told me, "My self-doubt of not being good enough holds back my power."

YES. So let's access that power.

I already addressed negative self-talk, but another huge necklace knot that needs to be untangled before we can embrace our power is WORRY. Worry is Fear's Executive Assistant, who runs its affairs with an unruly artfulness that keeps our minds entrenched in a relentless cycle. Worrying about doing something perfectly, worrying about whether people like us, worrying about failing, worrying if we're good enough. The cycle spins and spins, spiraling into assumptions and false beliefs faster than we can keep track.

Not only can worry falsely manufacture threats, but very slyly, it can also give us a feeling of perceived control. By worrying about every possibility, I often feel like I'm doing something to create the outcome I want. But the truth is that I'm usually powerless over the things I'm worrying about, and I'm simply functioning from a place of fear and imaginary control.

*One thing that is in my control? The choice to indulge the worrying.*

When I started to free myself a bit from worrying, I soon realized that so much time and energy are wasted on worrying. It dominates a teenage girl's brain in so many ways. *The Confidence Code*'s research found that three out of four teenage girls worry about failing.[3] In respect to body image, one study reports that at age 13, 53 percent of American girls worry about their body and are unhappy with it, and then this number grows to 78 percent by the time the girl reaches 17.[4] I'm needing that horror-stricken emoji again, because seriously, I HATE THESE STATS!

In working with girls, I try to dismantle these worries and fears by getting to the root of them. That could be figuring out whose mean self-talk voice she's listening to, or it could be a discussion about the worst-case scenario, where her fear usually lands in two primary buckets:

1. I won't be successful.
2. No one will love me for who I really am.

I bring these core fears into the light, without judgment, and we sit with them. And then, we accept them. A book on teenage girls would not be complete without a quote from Taylor Swift, who once wisely said, "Fearless is having doubts. Lots of them. To me, fearless is living in spite of those things that scare you to death."[5]

Taylor Swift is a great example of a woman who has stepped into her power, owning and accepting her doubts and fears. These insecurities are a part of life—a part of being human—and while they will always exist, we still have to choose to move forward. It takes courage, the type that's ready to confront *psychological* risk. Maybe we fear a physical attack from the bad guy waiting for us in the dark alley, but I think the psychological fear of failure or the fear of being unlovable are actually much more severe and pervasive.

We need to activate psychological courage in order to embrace what I consider one of the main antidotes to self-doubt: Self-acceptance. The Berkeley Well-Being Institute defines *self-acceptance* as "an act of embracing all of your attributes, whether mental or physical, and positive or negative, exactly as they are."[6]

So why should we accept ourselves for who we are? This kind of challenge demands a lot of humility, honesty, and courage. Who wants to get into all that? Aren't we more motivated when we're pushing ourselves to be better? Beating ourselves up with self-doubt, pushing ourselves out of fear . . . these are the intense forces that will drive us to succeed! Right?!

Nope. Instead, they oftentimes create a ton of pain.

The National Institutes of Health notes that a "lack of self-acceptance is characterized by feelings of worthlessness, inadequacy, depression, self-blame and self-hatred."[7]

In contrast, self-acceptance has made me feel so much better about myself. I'm not trying to be something that I'm not. For me, self-acceptance has been the difference between "I like myself" and "I will like myself **if** I'm _____ or **if** I do _____."

Rather than the more elusive positivity of self-confidence, self-acceptance is easier to turn to when I'm in the clutches of self-doubt. I can't make such a quick jump because I need to create some love around my limiting feelings. Self-acceptance is gentle. I don't need to do or be anything to achieve it.

AND . . . Self-acceptance is powerful. It allows for time and energy to flow where it's supposed to, gently, without force. Power can also be gentle. Power can arise from a sense of peace and happiness with who you are.

Dolly Parton once said, "Find out who you are and do it on purpose."[8]

I saw this type of power arise from Addison when she was only 13 years old—a time when I witnessed her accept herself for exactly who she was. She was struggling with math and her self-doubt around it seemed all-consuming. She fiercely hated her math-self and it was spiraling into some dark places. In talking with both Addison and her mom, we decided to shift her energy and focus on accepting who she was, rather than who she wasn't. We weren't going to feed the voices of self-doubt. We permissioned Addison to release the grip of any messaging telling her that she's a "failure" in math, and instead, she could just accept that it's not her thing.

Addison embraced the idea, and in that time, I watched her courageously *accept* that her math grade was going to be lower than she wanted. I watched her *accept* her fear that this might put her on a different academic track. I watched her *accept* that she wasn't perfect at everything. I watched her *accept* that she had limited energy, so she had better make a choice on how to spend her time. From that ease of acceptance, clarity began to appear.

Addison is socially talented, that's clearly what *she is*. Her mom and I began to enthusiastically affirm that part of who she is, saying things like, "Addison, I love how you can befriend any stranger and charm any person who crosses your path." It was vocalized in the same way that I recommend giving compliments where a girl's uniqueness feels really seen and celebrated.

Addison also cares deeply about improving the world around her, which is another part of herself that she started to embrace. After learning about my involvement with the nonprofits OneKid OneWorld and Glasswing International and their educational programs in Central America, Addison decided she would host a fundraiser to help build a school with them. By embracing her social talents, Addison knew she would be great at hosting a party.

Without any type of pushing or forcing, Addison fearlessly planned and executed the most magnificent event, helping to raise $40,000 that went to building a school in El Salvador. With her fundraiser, she was able to impact an entire community's access to education.

One might assume that Addison's success also stemmed from her having access to people with money who could attend her event and donate. There is always truth to how privilege creates access, and Addison herself would be the first to admit that. That's another part of herself that she accepted, recognizing that she lived in a world with larger financial potentials. And with that, she made choices. Girls in that world don't often spend their time trying to build a school in El Salvador. She could have chosen to do nothing.

Instead, Addison spent her time every day after school walking into random stores in Beverly Hills and wooing the manager until they donated something for her silent auction. She carried a patterned briefcase holding a letter of intent, 501(c)(3) proof, and a color-coded Excel spreadsheet to track her donations. She single-handedly persuaded vendors to donate food and beverages, cheerfully explaining to them how they'd get marketing exposure and a tax write-off. She personally reached out to attendees to invite them and followed up many times to make sure they were coming. She connected with the head of the nonprofit, who traveled from El Salvador and attended the event because Addison wanted to better understand the community she was helping and solidify her partnership with the people who live in that community. Addison effortlessly used her interpersonal intelligence to inspire everyone around her to be a part of something bigger than herself. Her self-confidence was exploding.

During that time, she didn't think twice about her math grade. If we had worried and fretted about her math skills, none of this would have happened. It really didn't end up mattering.

By getting to be herself, feeling celebrated for her natural talents, Addison told me recently, "I remember feeling unstoppable, like I could do anything."

Now an adult, and with her relational talents in full gear, Addison is still making the world a better place. Instead of her confidence dropping the normal 30 percent by age 14, I witnessed a moment in her life where she wisely accepted herself for who she was, freed herself from self-doubt, and consequently, stepped into her power.

Sitting with self-doubt, naming fears, accepting all of the ever-evolving aspects of myself. . . these intertwined necklace knots have not been easy to untangle. However, for me, I've stepped into the work because I feel healthier when I'm in that space of growth, even if it's emotionally hard. In the trenches of exploring self-doubt, teenage girls like Jade have taught me that I shouldn't let people dull my sparkle. That said, I didn't even know what my sparkle was until I started accepting myself as I am, rather than trying to be someone I'm not.

When I asked Jade, "What would freedom from self-doubt look like for you?"

She replied, "Being unapologetically myself."

Yeeess. My doubt has been the voice of other people, not me, and when I align with my own voice, a feeling of liberation occurs. Other people's opinions and control over me became more and more inconsequential. Watching teenage girls make this shift in their own lives has helped me envision a more fearless world where we can all do this. Fearlessness can simply look like a daily choice to listen to your true, inner voice, and if it's asking you to sparkle, you let it sparkle.

**Self-doubt is the feeling of not knowing what's coming next, and the fear that feeling holds.** —VIOLA, AGE 14

---

+ The mean voice inside our heads, telling us we're not good enough, is not our true voice.

+ At the root of self-doubt is fear, which can be paralyzing, but asking yourself honestly—"Where does this fear come from?" "Whose voice is this?"—and engaging in conversations with loving curiosity can activate courage.

+ Worrying is perceived control.

+ Confronting self-doubt with judgment-free levity can foster a capacity for discomfort, which offers an opportunity for learning and growth.

+ Self-acceptance, embracing both positive and negative attributes, will help someone step into their full confidence and power.

## CHAPTER NINE

# FRIENDS

*I would rather walk with a friend
in the dark, than alone in the light.*[1]
—Helen Keller

'd die without my friends."

"Really? Die?" I respond with a slight arch of my eyebrows. Sixteen-year-old Mira nods calmly as her pensive eyes look up, searching her thoughts.

"They're the only people I can be myself around."

"What does being yourself look like?"

"I can be a mess, and they still love me."

Mira nailed it.

"Do you think dying is a bit dramatic?" I say without any judgment in my tone.

Mira smiles and nods in agreement.

"It's all about the drama. My friends can handle the drama."

I smile, as she inspires me to look at drama in a whole new light.

When describing teenage girls, adults use the word *drama* very negatively to cast a shadow on big feelings. "You're being dramatic" is a frame that communicates a teenage girl is being irrational and luxuriating in her pain. Essentially, adults who use this term are responding to a girl by judging her pain. Whereas a friend does not judge. A true friend can love and comfort her while she is completely unreasonable, outraged, somber, and grumpy.

I've found that grown-up friendships do not have the same reckless abandon of love and support that I see with the ride-or-die friendships of teenage girls. When I asked girls for their thoughts on friendship, it was actually quite amusing how many of them brought up their devotion in terms of death. Driving home the point, Jade texted me:

"My friends are people who make me feel safe and supported so I never feel alone. Teenage girls will literally fight to the death for each other, lol."

That's some drama, and I love it. Please note, this language doesn't indicate any actual, potential death happening; it reveals how hard it is to find language big enough to encompass the love and feelings that girls have for their friends. I see a teenage girl's "drama" as passionate feelings mixed with honesty, vulnerability, and courage, giving her inner life a voice.

I want to know what I can learn from this drama. How can I support this passion within myself and others? I'm not talking about a negative reactivity that tries to escape my own pain by creating pain elsewhere. Some people might call that "creating drama," and I want to be clear that the type of teenage-girl drama I'm discussing never intends harm. I'm talking about dramatic feelings for the people I love. I'm talking about a drama that expresses the innate wisdom of teenage girls, particularly that *we all have a deep need to feel loved as our authentic selves and that friends are a critical channel of that love, especially when we're feeling our most imperfect and broken.*

As much as we can build self-acceptance, it's also good (and human) to need help and support from other people. I grew up thinking that if I didn't need anyone else, or ask for help, and just did everything perfectly by myself, then I would be a success. The goal was to never need anyone, and that would be proof that I'm doing well in life. Self-sufficiency has been taken to extremes in our modern world, so much so that we're back to the conversation of putting on an inauthentic show that "everything's great."

Everything is not great. Not for anyone. Some things can be great. Even a lot of things can be great. But every single person on the planet is currently going through some type of struggle. And we can't, and shouldn't, endure it alone.

What does that support look like for teenage girls? One of the best examples I can give is the devotion of a sleepover or slumber party. Having quality time with even one friend for 24 hours can uplift the soul in dramatic ways. I wish for everyone the joy that teenage girls feel from simply having a friend by their side while eating, laughing, doing their hair and makeup, texting, doing homework, partying, crying, socializing, choosing an outfit, traveling, posting on social media, watching a movie, snacking, venting, sleeping, being silly, and so much more.

It's a level of quality time and intimacy that's rarely replicated in adulthood. The only events verging on its specialness are girls' trips and bachelorette parties, which are definitely considered special occasions that create memories for a lifetime. We're lucky if we experience one of those every few years. And why is that? Why do we wait to make this specialness and connectedness happen?

I've taken this lesson very seriously and have actually had a lot of what I call adult-lady sleepovers. We're not usually sharing a bed, because growing up does alter a few needs, but we're all-in for a night of quality time together. After a few hours of simply getting caught up on the facts of life, we shift into that next, deeper layer. That's when the magic happens, and we share the messiness of our lives with one another.

Sleepovers provide the time to let emotional walls collapse, so that the mess can be revealed. It takes tons of love and care before we feel like it's safe enough to be vulnerable. While hanging out on FaceTime together, Madelyn shares her observations with me about why she thinks this level of connectedness is rare among adults:

"Adults are expected to have it all figured out, but age doesn't define your struggles. Everyone needs people to lean on. I think the pressures and expectations put on adults make them less vulnerable and honest with each other."

It feels like this 17-year-old has it more figured out than most of the adults I know. Not to underestimate her wisdom, Madelyn goes on to tell me that she feels so authentic with her friends that the type of love they share makes her often feel like she's "in love" with them. Her tone is so openhearted and at peace when she speaks that it catches me off guard. How wonderful to love and feel so loved by a friend, even when you're a mess.

I don't see a lot of adults actively sharing their mess, and it's certainly been something that's felt foreign and scary to me. I've rarely been a full-blown mess in life, but the moments that I've experienced a full state of brokenness have actually been the most important of my life. Two years ago, I underwent multiple surgeries, and my doctor had to put me on a full month of strict bed rest while some of the most profoundly sensitive parts of my body tried to heal, which extended into months of excruciating pain.

I was a MESS. For the first time, in a big way, I had to ask for help. It felt like tearing off my skin. In many ways, asking for help was more painful than the surgery itself, which was a huge lesson I needed to learn from that experience.

It was so uncomfortable to be in a place of need. Teenage girls, on the other hand, are very open about *needing* their friends. And when they communicate that need, their friends *show up*. When I asked Hazel about the importance of her friends, a look of unconditional love washed over her.

"My friends have curled my sobbing body. I've had moments where I couldn't stop crying, and they just held me."

It looked as if Hazel was being held as she described this. She's teaching me that if I'm brave enough to be vulnerable, potentially sobbing in need, it's a friend who can deeply show up for me in comfort. I might just need to ask for help first.

Eighteen-year-old Nora tells me, "Teenage girls can share their mess with a friend because they know she isn't going to judge them. We know it's the reality of life that things can be messy. We don't feel the need to hide that."

I've incorporated that wisdom into my life by intentionally saying out loud to my friends that I'll be there for them. I reinforce that we're on the same team as we face life, and that as teammates, we're going to be called to celebrate wins and also hold each other through losses. I voice this to my friends with the devotion of a teenage girl who will FaceTime with a friend for hours to discuss how a crush liked an Instagram post and what that could possibly mean. I want my friends to know that if it matters to you, it matters to me.

It's important to note that I'm not talking about codependency, which is defined as "a psychological condition or a relationship in which a person manifesting low self-esteem and a strong desire for approval has an unhealthy attachment to another often controlling or manipulative person."[2]

I'm talking about a devoted Friendship Love that shows up for the mess. I wonder if we permissioned ourselves to embrace our inner drama a bit more, maybe we'd become more familiar with our emotions, and they wouldn't feel so frightening.

When I talk about teenage girls' Friendship Love with adults, they usually respond with, "But girls are so mean to each other! What about the cliques and the gossip?"

Engaging this conversation has been another important area of healing for my inner teenage girl. With previous generations, girls have been hearing the message that there's limited space at the table for women, usually only one job/promotion/award set aside for one woman. Ranging from career success to male attention, we were taught to compete. The movie *Mean Girls* seemed to encapsulate the issue with the pain and ridiculousness that it deserved, and now, thankfully, this is one of those stories that's visibly dying out.

There's a new movie in town, and it's called WOMEN SUPPORTING WOMEN. The mainstream narrative is finally starting to tell girls that it's cool to passionately celebrate and help other women, and it's healing my inner teenage girl who was taught to compete with women. This frame of mind is developing in places that might surprise you, like social media. Wait, what? Isn't that where girls tear each other apart and spiral into a world of bullying and insecurity? I will dive more into this surprise in the chapter The Media, but 15-year-old Rosy specifically says that social media has helped her.

"I see lots of TikTok videos of girls supporting girls, which inspires me to support girls. In the comments on social media, girls uplift each other with lots of compliments and emojis. We also defend each other if needed and give a vibe that's like, 'You go girl, you got this!' "

The collective tone has shifted: It's a lot less cool to be mean and a lot cooler to be encouraging and compassionate. With Gen Z's focus on mental health, they've ushered in a new cognizance around everyone's struggle. Can girls still be mean to each other? Of course, because we're still imperfect human beings. However, in supporting girls through a "mean girl" situation, the conversation often goes something like this, where I ask about the girl being mean to her:

"What do you think that girl's home life is like?"

"I actually know that her dad is a jerk. And her mom criticizes her all the time."

"Wow, what do you think about that?"

"I think it's probably really awful for her."

"Do you think that affects her behavior toward you and other girls at school? Do you think she might be functioning out of a hurting and insecure place?"

"Yeah, she's not happy."

"Do you think she's trying to make herself feel better by trying to make herself seem superior to other girls?"

"That's exactly what she's doing. . . . Ah man, that sucks for her. I feel bad that she's going through that."

Folks, that's compassion and empathy at its finest. And today's teenage girls are good at it! When guided with care and emotional safety,

I've found that today's girls are a lot less judgmental of each other and a lot more accepting of differences. They've inspired me to be louder in supporting my women friends with a "You do you" enthusiasm. I've also found that instead of being sucked into the lowly vortex of gossip, I'm now framing the people around me with understanding and care. When someone tries to gossip with me, I often respond with something like:

"We're all just functioning the best we can out of the normal wounding of life. Let's cut her some slack."

That wounding often stems from our familial life, so that's another reason it's absolutely critical to have a world of love, apart from family, to support us. When teenagers face trials in life, research shows that being with friends produces "lower sadness, worry and jealousy compared to being alone, and lower sadness compared to being with family."[3] For teenage girls, supportive friends offer more relief from the pains of this world than family does. Bella, who I consider really close to her family, described this for me when she shared:

"My friends are different than my other relationships, like my mom or my sister, because they can understand me in ways others can't. Even though friends can be complicated, I feel like they bring me the most joy. I wouldn't be able to thrive or get through anything without my best friends to support me."

Bella highlights the truth of feeling like friends understand us better. I subscribe to that, as do many of us, and I think there's a great deal of magic in the fact that friendships are *chosen*. Like others, I often call my friends my Chosen Family. I feel a sense of obligation with Family Love, so when I show up for those hard times, it's not always as pure of heart. My heart is much more open when there's a choice, and friends are truly one of those choices in life that I can fully own.

With teenage girls, they often feel a pressure from their family to develop into what adults think is best. It's very rare for a girl to feel like she can be fully herself because families, and the dynamics around them, carry a lot of baggage, past histories, and personal agendas.

A friend should have no agenda. If you do find yourself with a friend who clearly wants to change you, then I would head in a different direction, as soon as possible. When a girl is struggling with a friend who is coming up short, I often ask her with a loving, nonjudgmental, curious tone:

"Why is she your friend?" We will often talk through the intellectual idea of having choices. With friends, we have a choice, so it's important to know why we're choosing to have that friend in our lives. I'll often further the conversation with:

"Do you like yourself when you're around her?"

Additionally, when a girl is struggling with "finding her people," we talk about how she can first be more boldly herself. I'll expand on how to discover that more in the chapter Identity, but the idea is to be the type of person, the type of friend, she would want. When she's that person first, she'll more naturally attract those types of friends who she'll consider "her people." I find that when she's obsessing about trying to fit in or be "normal" or "cool," her sense of self becomes diluted and disconnected. Most importantly, we focus on finding the people who love us exactly the way we are, so much so that Madelyn would say they're "in love" with you.

Taking all of this to heart, I ended up theming my bachelorette party as a teenage girl slumber party. Me and twelve grown-ass women slept on air mattresses in my friend's living room, braided each other's hair, did facials, played truth or dare, laughed, then laughed some more, and talked deep into the night, about all of life. It was a blast. Recently, my best friend, Bailey, themed her fortieth birthday party similarly, having her friends wear pajamas, enjoy a cookie dough tasting, get psychic readings, and sing karaoke until 1:30 a.m. Why? *Because we can.* Seriously, why not? The memories from these nights are profoundly full of a heartfelt, playful, vulnerable Friendship Love.

Playfulness is the best antidote I've found to alleviate pressure, expectations, and anxiety. Walls come down when people are laughing, and when people feel safe, they are more likely to reveal who they truly are. And when the laughter calms down and there's a moment where a friend shares how they're struggling, then wonderful. Our hearts are open and at ease, ready to cushion their vulnerability with love.

Learning these lessons from witnessing teenage girls' friendships, I now intentionally make so much time for my friends in my life. I tell them that I'm all in, and I invite their drama. Not a drama where people are fighting and throwing ego tantrums. I invite the drama that's stirring their souls in all directions—light, dark, and certainly the gray.

It's the drama where our humanity exists. It's the drama of a devoted love that says, "You're not going to go through this alone."

My friends don't judge me for anything, which makes me feel accepted.

—CHARLEE, AGE 14

---

✦ Adults could learn from the ride-or-die devotion of teenage girls' Friendship Love by learning to cultivate more intimacy and vulnerability in their own friendships.

✦ Gen Z's focus on mental health and gender equality has started to shift the narrative around girls' friendships toward compassion and encouragement rather than meanness and competition.

✦ Rather than dismissing and judging a teenage girl's sense of drama, we could learn from how she passionately shows up to support her friends during the messy times of life.

✦ Teenage girls' friendships show us how asking for help and needing each other is not a weakness or imperfection, but rather an important part of being human.

✦ Longer amounts of quality time with friends, similar to a teenage girl slumber party, can be a source of connectedness that allows emotional walls to collapse and vulnerable connections to grow.

# CHAPTER TEN

# THE MEDIA

*I think if women are visible in the media,*
*truly visible, in an empowered role, it empowers us*
*to be more visible in any area of our lives.*[1]
—Jane Fonda

The world is undeniably shouting at a teenage girl about who she *should* be, what she *should* be doing, and how she *should* be doing it. Until we release the strangling hold that these "shoulds" have around her neck, it's going to be hard for her to step into her own potential. Perhaps we underestimate a teenage girl because we can simply look around and see the whole world conspiring against her liberation and authenticity.

I'm not quick to make the media the entire villain of this story. I hope to explore the complexity of our seemingly limitless world. For this conversation, I'll consider the media in partnership with our culture, where the messaging from social media, movies, TV, news, books, brands, music, magazines, fashion, celebrities, advertisements, and the endless supply of content on the internet is pummeling our brains like never before in history.

It's wildly difficult for an adult to navigate this onslaught, so certainly the strain on a teenage girl is monstrous. In order to face that cultural monster bravely, I dive into media literacy conversations with an inquisitive zeal. "Media literacy" is just a boring way of saying I talk a lot about TV shows, celebrities, and stuff that seems superficial, but it's really not.

Research shows that teenagers engage with some form of media for about seven and a half hours EVERY DAY, and on average, over three hours of that is spent watching television.[2] Ranging from *Grey's Anatomy*, to *Wednesday*, to *Bridgerton*, to *Dickinson*, to *Riverdale*, to *The Kardashians*, some of my most revealing conversations have occurred when we're talking about who-loves-whom or who's-right-or-wrong on a TV show.

I particularly love talking about Kim Kardashian . . . Cue the eye roll from most adults I know. If you're still stuck on the eye roll when it comes to Kim Kardashian, then you're probably missing out on a dynamic world of conversation with teenage girls. Kim's life and persona spark so many interesting perspectives from girls. We can discuss Kim's body, whether it promotes plastic surgery or has ushered in a new era that celebrates curves. We can talk about her career, whether we support her selling shapewear or admire how she's working to become a human rights attorney. We can talk about her wealth, which can feel disconnected from the real world, or we can talk about how she fiercely uses her resources to free incarcerated people from death row. Even if you disapprove of how she rose to power, Kim is still undeniably one of the most influential women on the planet. And when adults roll their eyes at her, teenage girls see that judgment actively degrading, invalidating, and demeaning a powerful woman. However, when a girl gets to openly discuss Kim's many layers, without judgment, she explores and develops her own perspective that often wisely reflects the nuance.

If there's ever a tone of judgment during these conversations, then they'll shut down quickly. That would be a shame, because I'm telling you, *this is the way in.* The media offers a really easy access point to bring up topics with teenage girls that would feel forced otherwise.

I take the plunge into the sparkling media pool with girls every day, and I'm going to be bold (and maybe controversial) and say there is so much untapped, *positive* potential that exists within it. Over the years, I've learned from teenage girls that *the media helps us develop our identity and values, and by mindfully engaging in conversation around it, we can learn from it and release the control it has over us.*

This is easier said than done, but I'm here to provide some tools to move forward. Most importantly, I don't want people to run away from these types of conversations. I encourage you to dive into the hard questions that don't necessarily have easy answers.

Which brings us to the moment everyone has been waiting for! It's time to talk about the number one teenage-girl-topic that adults ask me about: social media! Adults usually approach this subject with a tone of absolute certainty that it's the devil. There is *so much* talk about how "likes" and overly filtered beauty influencers are destroying the mental health and confidence of young women. Of course, there is truth to the toxic effects of thinking that everyone on social media is prettier, happier, and more liked than you. I'm not underestimating the alarming research that suggests how social media can change the brain development of young teens over a three-year period, noting "the brains of adolescents who checked social media often—more than 15 times per day, became more sensitive to social feedback."[3] That's not good news.

That said, there is a TON of focus on the harmful effects of social media, and I'm personally maxed out on reading about it. Rather than vilifying all of social media, fighting a futile war against it, and complaining that it's a cesspool destroying everyone, I've spent a lot of time asking girls for their thoughts on the situation. Because guess what? Social media is 100 percent here to stay.

I've been figuring out some ways to swim through what I wouldn't call a cesspool, but rather a complicated ocean. There are people who have managed to take advantage of the good parts of the ocean without drowning or getting eaten by a shark, so I'm thinking we can try to do that too.

Fifteen-year-old Waverly couldn't wait to share her thoughts on social media with me. Identifying as multiracial, pansexual, and a makeup-loving feminist, Waverly felt like her interests and identity were never represented in the older, traditional models of media like magazines. She wants all of us to know:

"Women have been comparing themselves and dissecting their looks *forever*, way before there was social media. But now, girls can take the power back by posting what makes them feel good and powerful. I can find topics and representation that inspire my best self on social media. We have choices. We have choices about who we follow, what to post, and I need everyone to know that we're smart enough to engage those choices."

Waverly makes a great point, because in my experience, we have been profoundly underestimating teenage girls' ability to navigate these choices in a positive way. I'm not saying that all girls are accomplishing this, I'm saying that we need to support them with tools to accomplish this. That type of engagement takes conversation, genuine interest, and *respect*. I find that girls are very aware of adults' concerns and *want to be part of the conversation*.

I know many girls who have actively chosen to limit their engagement because they've felt that the pressures on appearance are too much. They chose it, no one forced them to do it. I haven't seen success come from efforts to control or force rules. When I see a girl being yelled at to get off her phone, I see resistance, disconnection, and resentment flare up. Instead I ask, "What Instagram and TikTok accounts have been inspiring you lately?" Then a conversation opens up and I'm wowed by the answers.

I've found that the teenage girls I know love accounts that cover mental health, body image positivity, feminism, LGBTQ+ rights, psychology, art, and racial justice. They love when I recommend the accounts that are inspiring me, and overall, I find that they're very open to having a diverse feed of visuals, interests, and education. I'll dive into the body image conversation on social media more in the chapter Beauty, but Waverly thinks the stereotype that teenage girls are obsessing over the model's skinny body is really discounting a lot of opportunities to change the entire dynamic of social media scrolling.

She tells me, "People think social media is undermining mental health, but it's actually helped mine. I follow a lot of accounts that have given me life-changing therapy tips, like how to ease anxiety and how to have better communication in relationships. Also, when I was younger and dealing with some internalized homophobia, social media was the only place where I felt like I could be myself. I found a supportive LGBTQ+ community of teenagers across the country who helped me come out. Without that, I don't know how long I would have struggled alone in silence."

Many girls have told me similar stories, wherein social media provided them with an opportunity for exploration and self-discovery that they wouldn't have gotten in their day-to-day world.

However, I know that a greater exposure to the world creates concerns, one of which is online bullying. Again, I think we're underestimating a girl's ability to confront these challenges. Adults often take a black-and-white approach, like "That's bad, make it go away." But what if we asked the girl:

"What do you think the solution is to online bullying? How could you use your voice and power to push back against this problematic issue?" Girls shared with me:

"People think we're just getting bullied and then depressed, but girls these days stand up for themselves. Not only do we block those accounts right away, but we take screenshots and report them. If it's someone we know, we'll screenshot and post it, so our community can see who's bullying, and they can't hide."

From what they tell me, it's pretty badass. However, the girls who I see doing this have been encouraged by their family and friends, starting from a very young age, to use their power and voice. In contrast, when she's being told by everyone around her that she's a helpless victim of the evils of social media, I observe a girl who feels a lot less empowered to make smart choices. I've found that her ability to intellectually question the world around her needs to be activated. When I'm discussing a post that could spark a girl's insecurity, I usually just start by asking her, "Does that look real or fake to you?"

She often replies:

"Oh, that's fake. She used Facetune," or "Her body might actually be like that, but that's an unrealistic standard."

I love her authoritative tone on these matters. I respectfully respond, "Yeah, agreed, that's so smart you can see that." She smiles at my response, standing a little taller in her power.

This opens up the next layer of conversation. If you're worried about a girl negatively comparing herself to others on social media, then I encourage you to *ask her about it*. Adults often need to slowly build trust to get to conversations like these with girls, but it's worth it. With a laid-back, intellectual, genuinely curious tone that's not hunting for a specific answer, I ask a teenage girl, "Do you think this photo reflects that girl's real life?"

She usually answers, "I don't know, probably not."

"It's pretty perfect looking. She's so happy and gorgeous. Do you think it makes girls feel bad about themselves to see photos like this? Does it make you feel bad?"

"Sometimes." This reply is the door cracking slightly open for a deeper conversation. I never want to jump in too soon, so I try to get into the mess of it all with her, calling out my own participation in this mess:

"I've done that, you know. Posted a photo that felt happier than my current truth. It didn't feel good. What do you think of that? Am I lame? You can judge me for it."

Girls often laugh when I invite their judgment, and laughter always helps create ease. With care for me, she'll often say, "I think we all do it. It can be hard not to."

"Yeah, I agree. I'm so glad you have awareness around it. That's really smart."

I know there are also valid concerns around social media's

algorithms, which are created to be addictive, and again, I engage her intellectual thoughts on it and ask her directly:

"Do you think there's an addictive property to social media?" She usually answers yes, and then I follow up with:

"What do you think the solution is? How do you feel like you navigate that in a healthy way?"

When conversations like these naturally expand, I make sure that I'm always listening closely to what she cares about and asking questions to better understand. With any concerns, I encourage parents to simply ask her about it with a tone of respect that seeks to understand and factor in her voice. I try to keep my focus on empowering her with trust that she can navigate the social media landscape, which consequently helps her trust herself more, because an adult is telling her that she's smart and capable.

I've found that by slowly opening up conversations with a completely nonjudgmental tone, so many significant topics can be explored. Recently, a girl severely struggling with burnout shared a TikTok montage with me that helped her express her intense feelings, which opened the door for us to talk about them. Another girl shared an infographic with me on the different trauma responses and how she had known about fight or flight, but that learning about the freeze response, where a person can become physically immobile, has helped her so much in better understanding a traumatic event that she experienced.

Obviously, girls shouldn't rely solely on social media for mental health information, but we're underestimating what a great starting point it can be. All types of media offer us a portal into crucial conversations.

When the TV show *13 Reasons Why* came out on Netflix, it exploded in popularity among teenagers. All of my girls were talking about it, and I knew that I had to get into the conversation fast. The show is about the thirteen reasons why a teenage girl commits suicide.

For obvious reasons, the show can be quite controversial, as people worry that it glamorizes suicide. A study also made a connection to an increase in suicide among teenage boys during the month the show premiered. There is no way to know if there's a direct link, but of course that's a tragedy in all respects. In contrast to teenage girls, I've found that teenage boys are way less likely to talk about their personal issues and feelings with even a friend let alone an adult. That again is a topic that deserves a focus all to itself as we deconstruct the constraints of masculinity and work to change that narrative. I'm certainly an adult who is trying very hard to learn what type of media opens up more discussions and possibilities for boys.

In respect to girls and *13 Reasons Why*, I specifically witnessed them use it as a pivotal conversation starter for not only critical topics like suicide but also sexual assault, which the show covers with a great deal of intensity. I was able to hold space for their concerns around friends threatening suicide, and I was asked for more help and advice than usual. While the show sparked both constructive and triggering reactions, overall, I found they were learning how crucial it is to ask for help. By talking about it, they were learning that they're not alone in their pain.

These aren't topics that are just brought up out of nowhere. I've found that difficult conversations happen when they're sparked by an impetus. This could be an argument, personal pain, a deadline, or simply a TV show. A good starting point is to simply ask a teenage girl what her favorite TV show is and then watch it yourself. Don't make a big deal about it. Try to genuinely enjoy the show and then tell her what you like about it (not what you don't like). This will open unexpected doors if you just let the conversation expand naturally in an affirming environment.

Without discussion and intentionality, it is indeed much easier to become a victim of the manipulations of a culture focused on profit, physical beauty, and fear of not being enough.

As much as I've emphasized that girls can make smart, empowered choices, we need to make sure that we're giving them a world filled with *smart, empowering options*. We might be living in a new era of "You do you," but I also need to highlight that we're unfortunately still failing to create more empowering "you"s in the entertainment industry for young women to emulate.

There is still a dearth of women, older women, women with different body types, and LGBTQ+ and BIPOC characters with complex storylines in our TV shows and movies. For women specifically, a rule, commonly called the Bechdel Test, has been popularized to evaluate films.[4] To pass the test, a movie must have:

1. At least two named women in it
2. Who talk to each other
3. About something besides a man

To this day, our movies are shockingly failing this test, whether it's a Disney movie, an Oscar winner, or a woman-led film. I encourage everyone to check out www.BechdelTest.com to look up your favorite films to see if they pass. Of the 10,056 films in their database as of June 2023, only 57.07 percent meet all three conditions.

Can we please take a minute to recognize how bonkers this is? Not only are barely more than half the films passing, but also this assessment is the BARE MINIMUM standard. Apparently, it's difficult to make a movie that includes two named women characters who talk about something other than a man. This shit is ridiculous and enraging.

As box-office hits continue to fail the Bechdel Test, women are still being defined by their relationships to men.

Being defined by a man goes hand in hand with objectification because it separates a woman from her own individual value as a human being. Additionally, being defined by a man increases the sexualization of girls and women. Research shows that Black girls in particular are hypersexualized.[5] Whether it's conscious or unconscious, the collective socialization of manhood teaches boys and men to value women's body parts in terms of their sexual worth, which objectifies her and fails to consider her brain, personality, character, and humanity. It's angering, not because sexuality is bad, but because the media is warping a teenage girl's participation in identifying and embracing her own sexuality.

A girl's options to find role models in the media certainly hit another alarming wall when we look at the grip the media has on BIPOC representation. According to the Annenberg Diversity Report on Diversity in Entertainment, on streaming platforms, 37 percent of the shows have ZERO Black characters with a speaking role and 63 percent have ZERO Asian characters with a speaking role, male or female.[6] In American entertainment, white characters have always been considered "the norm," which has created a world where whiteness dictates our media exposure.

With the media telling girls what they should and shouldn't be, the possibilities are muzzled by a disgraceful history of centering whiteness, sexism, homophobia, and objectification. We need expansive options— and conversations around the complexity of those options. All leading to a discovery of personal identity and values.

Waverly tells me that she's tired of googling "what are some TV shows with positive LGBTQ+ representation" and only getting the few options she's already watched. When she excitedly told me to watch *Young Royals* on Netflix, I sat down to watch it and immediately started laughing out loud when I learned that it's a Swedish show. Teenagers are watching TV shows with subtitles! They're needing to find options in different countries because we're not showing up for them enough in the United States. At least, I can recognize that this is a positive example of how today's media landscape can provide new levels of access. I certainly couldn't access a subtitled Swedish show when I was growing up. But overall, I don't want them to have to work so hard to find and engage new options.

To create new options, it requires that we collectively recognize our power and make new choices. We can't simply buy into whatever is being sold. This starts with all the little choices.

Unfortunately, it usually takes less effort to buy into the media narratives that swirl around us. It usually feels easier to do what everyone else is doing. Buying the expensive face moisturizer feels easier to me because my friends are using it, and oh my gosh, what if I'm the only person who is dramatically aging?! It's harder for me to really think about and discuss what "aging" means to me. When I follow and buy into the culture, I do it because it feels like I'm being "normal." It feels that way because the media is putting on a spectacular circus that is distracting and dazzling me from every angle. And everyone I know seems to be participating in the circus! This makes it very hard to find the Exit.

I got some clarity on how to exit the circus by watching 16-year-old Raya. I've known her since she was eight, and even then she seemed like a hilarious, wise 70-year-old. When she identified as queer at age 14, she got herself an elaborate cake in the shape of:

A closet door with a rainbow shooting out of it.

And then she threw herself a party.

Raya has always done things her own way, naturally rejecting the mainstream culture around her. She's a wildly talented artist, so creativity flows through her with such a stunning force that she can't even imagine buying into the boring buzz of "normal." Raya's creative spirit is always breaking some type of rule, whether it's drawing doodles all over her desk in permanent ink or wearing two different color socks because she feels like it. Thankfully, her parents encourage her to embrace her kaleidoscope of individuality, so she has become even more confident and joyful in her expression. Throughout history, artists have always been leading the charge in bucking the system.

Raya inspires the part of me that loves to break the rules—the type of societal rules that fuel the circus and tell you that you're not pretty/skinny/smart/funny/kind enough, but if you buy this or do this, it will "help" you.

When I ask Raya how to find the Exit out of the media's circus, she told me, "Don't care what people think."

I love her ease with it. Unfortunately, it's not easy, but Raya has helped me see how it is *a choice*. When I care what people think, it's usually because I'm aligning myself with some media narrative or societal rule of what's "cool." However, Raya defines her own cool. When I choose to define my own sense of cool, it feels like I'm releasing the control that toxic cultural narratives have had over me.

Thankfully, I can now recognize that my mom has always pushed me in this direction. When I chose to wear a purple exercise sweatband for an entire year in elementary school, my mom glared at what she called "those judgy moms" and fiercely proclaimed, "She can wear whatever she wants!"

When I was planning my wedding, she told me, "I don't care if you wear combat boots walking down the aisle."

I haven't given my mom enough credit for those societal subversions that she planted in my heart. I feel much more whole, and honestly cool, when I'm not caring about the shiny billboard of the media circus. And instead, I'm just being my authentic self—an authenticity that rocks a *very cool* purple exercise sweatband.

The Identity chapter will further delve into finding one's authentic sense of cool, but here I want to encourage an identity exploration that's working to sever the media's control. Just like the teenage girls who dive into complex media literacy conversations with me, it's all about *questioning*. When I boldly question the societal rules that the media is feeding me, I find myself becoming more conscious of choices.

We can perform in the media circus like a well-trained animal, or we can question:

How are the animals being treated?

Why are the tickets to the show so expensive?

Can Janelle Monae star in the mainstage show instead of Carrie Underwood?

How much is the staff getting paid?

Are there as many performances by women as men?

Are there types of people not getting to perform at all?

If you're going to participate in the circus, I just want you to have as many options as possible, which might mean using your voice to advocate for some changes. People like to stay the same because it feels safe, but I've come to learn that the status quo is a metal chain of "You *should* _____" tied around our necks, choking us into silence. It's up to us to find the bolt cutters to set ourselves free.

If I had the power to improve our media and culture, I would make it more accepting and inviting for all different types of voices. —GISELLE, AGE 15

---

✦ Media literacy conversations that stem from things like TV shows, celebrities, social media, or movies can help a teenage girl discover her identity and values.

✦ Rather than vilifying all of social media, you can create the type of conversations that critically question societal narratives, while also empowering a girl to explore, learn, use her voice, and make positive choices for herself.

✦ Don't underestimate a teenage girl's ability to have intellectual conversations around the difficult topics that the media brings up.

✦ In order to expand the current, limiting messaging of what girls "should" be, we need to be creating media that empowers all types of women, and advances BIPOC and LGBTQ+ representation.

✦ It's important to recognize our power to make new choices that don't simply buy into the status quo.

## CHAPTER ELEVEN

# BEAUTY

*To be beautiful means to be yourself.*
*You don't need to be accepted by others.*
*You need to accept yourself.*[1]
—Thich Nhat Hanh

Yeah . . . you need to exfoliate your lips. I have this great sugar lip scrub that will scrape away the dead skin cells and help the lip balm moisturize better. Also, some ChapSticks are waxy. Let me show you brands that have quality moisturizing ingredients."

Lip scrub? So now I need to add that to the other 28 products I put on my face? This 16-year-old girl, who's helping me solve the URGENT problem of my cracking lips, nods emphatically. It turns out, she was one hundred percent right. My lips drastically improved after I implemented her plan. Obviously, we could be talking about much more critical issues, but somehow beauty always finds its way into the conversation.

If this book is about sharing the lessons I've learned from teenage girls, then we certainly could dive into beauty tips, because over the years I've learned a LOT! They know the ingredients in my moisturizers, shampoo, and face wash. They know what I should wear to an event, and how I should tilt my head for a photo. They often even know which products are cruelty-free and which fashion companies pay their international workers fairly or contribute to fast-fashion waste. They know the language of "beauty," but I try to make sure they also know whose voice and "authority" is defining this type of beauty.

Considering I spend time with a very diverse group of girls who represent different races, cultures, household incomes, and body shapes and sizes, it's absolutely critical that we identify the beauty standard of our society and media. Historically in America, it has been overwhelmingly heteronormative, white, thin, wealthy, young, able-bodied, and comes from Eurocentric ideals. If that messaging is saturating our media, then it would make sense why I encounter a lot of turmoil from girls who don't fit into those categories. Those beauty standards severely influence how we perceive ourselves when we look in the mirror.

This is the moment where I could easily and viciously tear into the beauty standards that annihilate women's self-worth. I could discuss at length how the pressures to be pretty govern a teenage girl's life, but that's a tired story. We already know that story. It's been the same old story for all of time. Beauty = Worth. A girl is told through movies, family, social media, men, books, models, friends, TV, and advertisements (and absolutely everything else) that if she is beautiful, then she has worth, and potentially, even power.

When I first started working with teenage girls, I was anti-beauty. I wasn't going to subscribe to that patriarchal bullshit! That meant barely any makeup, simple hairstyles, boring clothes, and lots of self-righteous superiority. I didn't need all that other crap because I was smart, kind, funny, generous, thoughtful . . . which is called INNER BEAUTY!!!!! I was shouting this because I thought that if I was loud enough, I would successfully hide my insecurities around my body and looks.

It was actually teenage girls who opened my eyes to a new world of beauty. One where everything doesn't have to exist in extremes. Girls will still readily admit that the media's beauty standards can make them feel like shit, but as usual, there's a much more nuanced conversation to be had.

Seventeen-year-old Riley notes, "It's complicated. We're all so taught to hate ourselves that it comes to a point where girls just need to do anything to feel okay about themselves."

So yeah, we put on a cute outfit, makeup, do our hair until we feel pretty, and for that moment it's true, we like ourselves more. That's not a bad thing. I really don't want to add new layers of shame to anyone's exploration of beauty. Some women and girls really love the process of beautifying themselves, some don't, and many fall somewhere in between. Everyone is welcome here.

Our society's obsession with beauty isn't going anywhere, so I've certainly needed to figure out a relationship with beauty that feels healthy. Teenage girls have helped me see how the journey can look different for everyone. The main lesson I've learned from them is that *if I let someone else determine what's beautiful for me, it'll bring me pain, so it's critical that I work to have my own unique, loving relationship with beauty.*

This process has taken a lot of engagement to start feeling serenity and wholeness around beauty. I've had to unpack all of the many voices (that weren't my own) that have been influencing me for decades.

One voice that I've witnessed to be particularly powerful on a girl's self-image is her mom's. My mom has always been very empowering and supportive of my looks, but I have two memories from my teenage years that still leave me wounded. Both times, I was showing her a new outfit, and she told me, "Suck in your gut."

Both times were a casual, quick moment, so my mom probably doesn't even remember them, but unfortunately, a teenage girl's brain is like a sponge when it comes to weight and body image. For many years, I had a lot of mental pain around my stomach not being flat enough. By no means should blame be put on my mom, because there were countless things that led to my disordered eating habits and obsessive thoughts about weight. I look at my mom with compassion and ask, "Whose voice was she listening to when she said that?"

Well, it's the same old story—the same old voice—with one addition . . . *Skinny* = Beautiful = Worth. Perhaps my grandma told my mom to also "Suck in your gut," because these patterns, stories, voices, and messages all get handed down to the next generation, usually unconsciously. We're all victims of the same system.

And yes, I use the word *victims*, because now is the time I bring up eating disorders again. I've already shared how common they are, but since writing the Perfection chapter, I was informed of yet another teenage girl in my life, whom I love and adore, and who has entered a treatment program for anorexia. Witnessing this struggle is an incredibly painful part of working with teenage girls.

Research shows that *over half* of adolescent girls engage in unhealthy weight control behaviors like crash dieting, fasting, skipping meals, hiding food, purging, overexercising, diet pills, or taking laxatives.[2] And to emphasize the stakes again, a girl is 12 times more likely to die if she has anorexia than a girl who doesn't have anorexia, because it is the most lethal mental health issue that exists.[3] And to broaden the scope, the University of North Carolina at Chapel Hill conducted a study that found that 75 percent of American women have struggled with disordered eating behaviors. Their findings cut across racial and ethnic lines, not limiting the issue to any specific group of women.[4]

Another difficulty is that society's standards around body weight change and it feels like we can never keep up. Today, a "thicc" body could also be interpreted as beautiful. A girl expressed frustration with me that she finally lost some weight and then was criticized for not having a bigger butt and curvier, fuller figure, which is considered "thicc." Whatever women or girls do, it never seems like enough. My friend Dr. Caroline Heldman, who is the chair of the Critical Theory and Social Justice Department at Occidental College and executive director of the Representation Project, started the very first college class in the U.S. named "Fatness," where so many of these topics are addressed. To explore the exhausting beauty landscape, we need more education and understanding on how to unpack these narratives.

I wish that I could offer some quick tricks on how to help girls with this, but this is where I redirect our collective finger to point at ourselves. At the end of the day, we can only heal ourselves, because we can't control society, the media, or any other human. Healing my relationship with my body has not been an easy journey. However, I can control my own language and attitude about my body when I'm in front of teenage girls.

I brought up moms earlier because they are usually the primary woman who is modeling behavior for teenage girls. To be very clear, I'm not saying moms are responsible for teenage girls' eating disorders. There are so many complicated factors that cause this issue. The moms I know who've supported their daughters through this struggle have been extremely mindful and caring in so many admirable ways.

I'm bringing up how the women in our lives model behavior because it's something girls have brought up with me—a lot. We can't control the media's harmful narrative around beauty standards, but we can control our own narrative. Unfortunately, teenage girls tell me that their moms, sisters, friends, teachers, and the women in their lives regularly comment negatively on their own bodies in front of them. Girls absorb that messaging, big time. I've personally witnessed a girl repeat the exact same negative phrasing that I heard her mom say. The words have gotten subtler over the years, which is progress, but they're still harmful. I used to hear a girl's mom say things about her own body like:

"I look fat in this," "Time for a diet, been eating way too much!" and "I'm so bad for eating this."

Now, it's a little more:

"I look big in these pants." "After the holidays, I need to start a new health kick!" "Sorry I look so bad right now" (which means no makeup), and "I shouldn't be eating this."

And then of course, there's a mom's commentary on her daughter's body:

"You're eating that?" "You lost weight! You look good!" "Let's stay healthy together and watch what we're eating." "That dress makes you look thin!"

I would be happy if all of these comments died an immediate

death. Some might seem innocuous, particularly the positive commentary about looking good, but believe me when I say, "Nope, big nope." I find that when girls and women hear a weight loss "compliment," they hear that their previous weight (and identity) was *baaad*. And skinny = good.

In general, I would recommend not commenting on a girl's body and encouraging her not to make comments either. You might think your comments are casual, but so often the impact adds to layers of shame. If there are concerns about a girl's eating habits and changing weight, I advise seeking professional guidance. Parents I've worked with have found helpful insight and guidance in Jennifer L. Gaudiani's book *Sick Enough*,[5] which emphasizes a common issue that a girl often doesn't think she's sick enough to warrant treatment even though her entire life is being negatively impacted. Overall, these are not issues to brush by or avoid.

I have had some positive discussions with girls when I use my approach of phrasing things as a question. However, with body image, I start in a different place that isn't personal, such as:

"What are your thoughts on the media's pressure to be thin? What do you think are the most toxic portrayals—models, actresses, ads?"

"What do you think would help women create a healthy relationship with beauty?"

"Where do you think the most severe pressures on body image and beauty come from?"

These types of questions give a tone of respect for their intellectual thoughts on the matter. I keep the tone very philosophical and genuinely curious. I love hearing their answers, because teenage girls have so many wise thoughts on this situation that need to be heard by us. In the following pages, I'll be sharing some of those thoughts, but I want you to know how ready they are for this type of conversation. They see it as a collective issue that we're battling against.

As 16-year-old Peeta describes: "I heard a guy say that clothes don't look flattering on plus-size models, and I thought, that's the mentality I'm here to defeat, both in myself and others."

In these conversations, I hold space for all their thoughts and feelings, reflecting what I hear, so they feel seen and understood. Oftentimes, after discussing the issues more intellectually, the conversation veers into the personal, and I hear more about their own struggles.

In an effort to never make girls feel alone in the messiness of life, I might share my own body image struggles. However, I don't share solutions that get me thinner. I share solutions that have helped me deconstruct the damaging narratives we encounter each and every day. Hope is important in this realm. Not the type of hope that's quick-to-fix or slapping positivity on a hard situation, but rather the type that's personal.

I find that if I share my own story, a girl will respond by asking the questions that she herself is grappling with, and therefore, guide her own process. I try really hard to never share with a tone of *I secretly hope you're learning the lesson I'm trying to teach.*

If I'm giving off even a slight hint of "You should do this," then the conversation shuts down.

I give hope in my story, because with a lot of hard work, I've broken damaging patterns. I've had to adopt a new level of mindfulness with not only how I speak and feel about my own body but also with how I interact with girls of all ages.

I had the gut-twisting realization when I read Lisa Bloom's viral article, "How to Talk to Little Girls," that there are so many subtle ways that I'm a part of the system that's perpetuating harmful narratives. Basically, the article asks:

*What's the first thing we usually say to a little girl when we see her?*

Most likely, it's about how cute she looks or the adorable outfit she's wearing. Whereas with boys, we often ask them what their favorite subject in school is or their favorite sport. I have 100 percent done this. I've repeatedly commented on a little girl's cuteness in the first few moments of interacting with her. Did I say it with good intentions, yes, but that doesn't take away from the message that it sends.

Bloom emphasizes that "teaching girls that their appearance is the first thing you notice tells them that looks are more important than anything." This messaging festers over time, as we unconsciously define a girl's "value" by whether she is pretty or not.

When I try to discuss this issue, I've had people specifically respond, "What?! Now I can't even tell a little girl she's pretty! PC culture is out of control!"

I'm not against telling a girl she's pretty, but if it's always the first and most frequent focus, then girls will get the message. When I hear this type of pushback, I ask:

"Why do forty-two percent of first- through third-grade girls want to be thinner? And by age ten, why are eighty-one percent of girls scared of being fat? Why is the current average age for a girl to start dieting age eight?"[6]

Those are some appalling statistics that we need to collectively reckon with. Clearly, eight-year-old girls are hearing the message. So back to the finger-pointing . . . Who's sending this message?

I've been trying really hard to unpack how I communicate this message in the world. If I want change, I need to start with myself. I believe that my own inner healing has had a positive ripple effect on the girls in my life. I've had to take a hard look at my relationship with beauty, and the wisdom of teenage girls has helped me evolve.

Olivia had an immediate answer when I asked her about her relationship with beauty:

"I like making myself feel pretty with things like fashion and makeup. I feel more confident afterward, but it's not where I get all my confidence. You have to have your own standards. Don't compare yourself."

Keisha further emphasized this idea of focusing on yourself:

"When someone tells me I look pretty, I ask, 'How do you define *pretty*? What does *pretty* mean to you?' I have to find my own answer to that. My self-worth isn't going to be determined by how society evaluates my looks."

The finger points back to herself. *She* gets to choose what's beautiful. I've learned from girls that fashion is a great place to start finding "your own standard." Fashion's expression of identity will be explored more in the next chapter, but your choices in clothes often also reveal your relationship with beauty. Back when I was anti-beauty, I wore simple outfits that I can barely remember. I was trying to tell the world through my clothes that I didn't care about beauty, which now I can see was not true. I cared, but I was scared of letting my beauty, which is unique to me, shine.

Teenage girls love to explore bold clothing choices and discuss how an outfit makes them feel. However, they're often overwhelmed with concerns about what people will think. I love discussing with them how this connects to the same people-pleasing pattern that shows up in other parts of her life. Returning to the lesson of that chapter, the only person who she can truly please is herself. Keisha has really embraced this and loves to assert:

"If people have a problem with an outfit I've got on because it's 'a bit much,' then that's their problem, not mine. I love how I feel in it, because it's connecting me to elements inside of me that are excited to be expressed."

Taking selfies is a good example of teenage girls experimenting with how beauty relates to their identity. I hear from adults that they think selfies are the poster child for vanity, superficial beauty, and the villainy of social media. I haven't found one teenage girl who agrees with that. I asked Giselle first, who I know to be a harsh critic of popular culture and who refuses to follow the crowd, but she still responded with:

"Selfies are just a fun thing that everyone does. Don't overthink it. Get over it, it's just a photo. It can be like a self-portrait, like art."

I found out that Giselle actually doesn't take selfies, but she thinks it's really unfair for adults to judge girls who like to, and she felt drawn to defend this misunderstood part of her generation.

Seventeen-year-old Lauryn really likes to take selfies, and she told me, "Selfies implement a source of self-power. If I take a picture of myself that I feel good enough about to post on social media, then it feels good. There is a sense of creativity and fun in selfies that the older generation isn't able to see. I use selfies to, yes, make sure I look good, but also to have fun with my self-image and increase my self-confidence."

I used to be really judgy of selfies, and now I take them, because these girls are right. I feel a sense of confidence emerge when I like a photo of myself—I don't need to overthink it. Teenage girls have also helped me look at the relationship between beauty and social media with new eyes. Yes, social media can undeniably perpetuate toxic narratives about beauty, but as I've noted earlier, girls are capable of questioning those narratives with the right type of engagement. When these conversations start at a young age, I've seen her grow into a young woman who can offer way more wisdom on the topic than grown adults who oversimplify it into a villain.

I think that completely restricting all access to social media underestimates teenage girls' intelligence to understand what's real and fake beauty. The discussion I have with girls is often around *appearances*. I'll ask for her intellectual thoughts on adding "beautifying" filters to an image, and we'll discuss, with no judgment. She knows that a smiling photo on Instagram could be masking darker truths, or it could be wanting to share something that makes a girl happy. How do we evaluate, for ourselves, what feels true and what feels like a mask?

Madelyn offers her thoughts. "You can tell when a post is for you and not for anyone else. Or it can be for you and also to empower others. It's more of 'We're all in this together. I'm a badass woman and so are you.' "

She's pointing out the *intention* behind the beauty that someone wants to share. I've noted how teenage girls are brilliant at spotting the truth, and when I've seen that skill empowered, girls perceive social media posts with depth and accuracy. Madelyn further notes:

"With social media, it's more than how you look, you're trying to make your whole life beautiful. But beauty is constantly changing. It's now more of what you're doing to feel a certain way in response to the world around you."

Feelings, yes . . . How does this photo/video/person make me feel? How do I feel when I post this photo of myself? The answer can be "It makes me feel powerful," but it can also come from a place of need, such as "I need to get a lot of likes on this in order to feel good about myself." If we talk about these things, being honest with ourselves about our feelings and intentions, then we start to really connect with our true, inner voice.

Fifteen-year-old Rosy tells me, "Beauty is feeling good on the inside and outside. It's transparency within yourself, not hiding, being real. I take a selfie when I'm feeling beautiful because it makes me feel confident, but I think it's beautiful when a girl posts a selfie crying because it shows that transparency. It shows that not everything on social media is perfect."

Sometimes, social media can be a positive aid in developing a girl's relationship to beauty. Girls love social media's clever posts dissecting the photoshopping and body altering that happens in national advertising campaigns and on magazine covers. It's thankfully becoming cooler for celebrities to call out the media for altering and retouching their images rather than blindly participating in it. That type of content isn't appearing in any other mediums. If you haven't yet seen a young woman on TikTok excoriate the beauty industry for altering images, then you're in for a treat. Do not underestimate young women's ability to shred toxic systems.

Additionally, there can be a really positive cultural exchange on platforms. Fourteen-year-old Tisha and her family come from Kenya, so she made sure that I understood:

"People in the U.S. see a lot of entertainment media with European beauty standards, but I like people who look like me, which I can find more of on social media." She went on to explain her definition of beauty that's been influenced by African culture, and she lit up from within excitedly sharing it with me.

There is certainly more representation on social media. I can't tell you how many teenage girls have told me that Lizzo's Instagram page has had a huge influence on them. Girls really feel the love that Lizzo has for herself, and they want that too.

Seventeen-year-old Hazel is biracial—half Black, half white—and she comments how TV has gotten slightly better in representing her, but people don't realize how much she's struggled with something as simple as her hair. She tells me how she used to spend two hours straightening it in order to "Conform to a beauty standard that I now know is impossible for me. The problem is that I got a LOT of compliments when I straightened my hair, but it never felt good, because it didn't feel authentic. I felt most seen when people asked me, 'Why didn't you leave it curly?' "

When Hazel was faced with that question, she had to find her own answer. Hazel has told me about her experience of listening to her inner voice, and how it's gotten stronger. She said, "I now feel the most internally beautiful that I've felt in a really long time. Before, I was so consumed with worry about what people thought of me. But now, I feel inner peace from listening to myself. Trusting myself to make decisions. Enjoying what I enjoy. That's self-love. I don't need other people to make me feel better."

When girls share wisdom like this with me, I affirm with enthusiasm, so they can feel the impact of their powerful and inspiring words. I make sure they know how much I admire them. I compliment their perspective, so that they can feel seen in moments when they are understanding life *beautifully*. With these thoughts, Hazel also introduces a new distinction.

I explored self-acceptance as the solution in the chapter on self-doubt, which I still think is absolutely critical. However, there's one more step we can take. It's a concept that will be experienced wildly differently by everyone—self-love.

There are plenty of cheesy narratives around the term "self-love" that I'm trying to avoid. When a concept is thrown around a lot as something that we're failing to do yet again—"You just need to love yourself more!"—then it can be hard to find an entry point.

Jade and I were caught in this conundrum, as she aptly pointed out, "The whole self-love approach where you say 'I'm a goddess' type of thing is great, but not achievable." Jade went on to stress how neutrality feels more achievable because we don't always feel like a goddess. She emphasized how there are lots of phrases and words like "inner beauty" that just don't resonate with girls.

Within this discussion, Jade and I were trying to figure out the language that worked in a new way for her, and she shared, "Beauty is knowing who you are. Walking through the world with your own light, which attracts other people's light. Beauty is about the energy you share."

Applause, for yet another wise teenage girl sharing her light with me. I like that she used the word *energy* because I think that it's a word that can often be more accessible and relatable for teenage girls. If I were to interpret what they mean when they use it (which is often), I would say it's quite similar to *love*.

Self-love can feel overwhelming, like if we're not doing it perfectly, then we're failing at it. I think an easier entry point is to share loving energy and see what type of feelings that creates inside you. I'm talking about a collective love for humanity and not a romantic love here. Saint Augustine nailed it when he wrote:

"Inasmuch as love grows within you, so beauty grows. For love is the beauty of the soul."[7]

Connecting with the beauty of your soul is highly individualistic. I can't tell you how to do that for yourself. But I see Hazel's listening and trusting herself, and Jade's energy that she shares with others as examples of this in practice.

I do know that when we turn the finger to point at ourselves, we must do it with love. Love is never characterized by judgment. I'm not evaluating my beauty, I'm discovering it with an open heart. I almost wrote the lesson of this chapter as finding a *healthy* relationship with beauty, but I realized that it's much larger than that. I've needed to find a *loving* relationship with beauty. French dramatist Jean Anouilh's words have always resonated with me:

"Things are beautiful if you love them."[8]

I've asked girls, "What are some ways you access that sense of love for oneself?"

Hazel shared, "My inner voice is connected to my inner child, and children usually understand love a lot better than adults."

This inspired me to ask my six-year-old niece, Lemon, what beauty means to her. She quickly pointed out the window and said, "That!"

I turned around and saw the most beautiful sunset happening over the ocean. I hadn't even noticed. Perhaps a lot of beauty is happening, but we don't see it because we're too focused on something else, something to fix because the world is loudly saying it's "ugly."

I looked at the sunset and smiled at Lemon. "That's beauty to you?"

She nodded and then looked at me with an absolutely pure, heartfelt honesty. "And me, and you, we're beautiful."

She said it with so much love and ease—not weighed down by society's messages telling her what beauty is or isn't. Looking through the eyes of a child opens up an expansive world of love where so many more things are beautiful.

This is what Hazel is talking about. She emphasized with me, "Children don't care about your weight or what makeup you're wearing. When I connect with my inner child, I'm connecting to my values and a higher sense of self."

When facing the daunting and damaging narratives around beauty, Hazel is reminding us that we can choose to stay connected to that loving, childlike, innocent beauty. It can be elevating, healing, and powerful. It's the type of power that can change the story around beauty for all of us.

**CORE INSIGHTS**

Beauty is your heart and the inside of you as a person. —PAISLEY, AGE 13

---

✦ People want to break free from oppressive beauty standards, but you already have the power to choose what you think is beautiful.

✦ Unpacking and questioning the many voices that influence your perception of beauty is critical because the pressure on body weight alone can create severe consequences.

✦ Teenage girls are capable of questioning beauty narratives, creating nuanced conversations that explore rather than judge.

✦ Teenage girls can shine light on how beauty is connected to love and the energy we share.

✦ If you let someone else determine what's beautiful for you, it'll bring you pain, so it's critical that you work to have your own unique, loving relationship with beauty.

## CHAPTER TWELVE

# IDENTITY

*Be yourself; everyone else is already taken.*[1]
—Oscar Wilde

W hen I first get on the phone with parents, before I've even met their daughter, 99 percent of the time they tell me something about her identity using very concrete language.

"She's an athlete, not a book reader." "She's an artist, not a math person." "She's a hard worker, not a go-getter." "She's a people person, well liked, but not disciplined with her time."

For tutoring, I'm often hired to help their daughter become . . . more of what she's not.

I've had experiences with girls growing into some new identities, but I've also fallen on my face, deeply learning how to better listen to a teenage girl's authentic quest for identity.

Even when parents accept that their daughter isn't the most academically inclined, they still adamantly want her to be productive. If I were to pop open a large umbrella that would stretch over all the identities that are raining down on teenage girls, I would say that the winner, where there is the greatest demand, is the identity of being productive. This shows up more than identities of being kind, perfect, generous, likable, or smart. Basically, everyone wants their kid "working hard." Not doing anything is simply not an option.

The Productivity Umbrella makes parents feel like it'll protect them and their daughter from the rainstorms of life because if you do, do, do and go, go, go, then at least there's a chance of "success." They're simply dialing into the cultural messaging that productivity is the safest bet to achieve the career and financial status that society is telling us we want.

Of course, I'm not against working hard, but I know what it's felt like to have that identity of being a Hard Worker dominate my choices. And then when my hard work didn't pay off with the expected success, I fell apart. My identity crumbled around this mentality, in what I've seen to be a common quarter-life crisis.

To fulfill the hardworking "American Dream" mentality, teenage girls pursue interests in which they're being affirmed. If they're naturally good at it, they'll continue to do it and do it more intensely. Teenage girls form a lot of their identity from the activities they're involved with, so it's important to understand the influences that guide them. Eighteen-year-old Davina has always shared her frustration with me that her peers can't explore lots of different interests, because if they're bad at it, then everyone tells them that they should stop doing it. She wisely connects the issue to the pressures put on women:

"Any time we talk about a successful woman, they have to be SO much better than any man in that field, which is crazy. They're so rarely recognized even if they're the best in their field, so it feels pointless for a girl to pursue something she's bad at. We're told it's a waste of time."

Davina sees a lot of doors shut for her peers because they're so scared of being bad at something. Not only does this tie into perfectionism, but it's also a mechanism for people-pleasing. Girls frequently pursue interests and develop their identity based on being good at something, even if they don't like it.

I also often witness a space where a teenage girl is exploring her identity, but nothing feels easy or the right fit for her. She's struggling to find herself. If a girl doesn't feel like she fits into the "normal" box or the established system of success, it can be particularly difficult. When

I asked teenage girls for topic ideas that they wanted me to cover in this book, Cynthia chimed in with a very popular response:

"Exploring my interests in the face of parental expectations."

They communicated that it was a huge stress for them. I've found that there's an enormous amount of power a girl can offer when she finds a path that lights her up, but they often feel held back by someone else's needs. Familial and social pressures can be very loud, and lots of times the pressure of productivity is so forceful that it's hard for a girl to recognize her own inner likes and dislikes. Consequently, I would love to give attention to how her identity is evolving and needs a ton of room to swing in seemingly messy and unexpected directions.

In particular, Gen Z *hates* to check boxes. It could be their style, sexual identity, career goal, really anything. I dare you to try to slap traditional, clear-cut labels on a girl born from 1997 to 2014. I absolutely love their fierce resistance because it shows their prescient understanding that humans live in a state of constant change and growth.

However, a huge issue confronting girls is that colleges like to accept students who have their identity nailed down. If this term wasn't overused enough, the college admissions world calls it their "brand." Do we brand a student as an athlete, a STEM kid, an activist, an artist . . . ? *What will you contribute to our campus community?*

This is the question every single college application asks, with the tone of a stressed-out FBI interrogator who is on his sixth cup of coffee. Cue: a teenage girl falling apart, as she struggles to figure out exactly who she is by the November first early-decision deadline.

I have the immense privilege of sitting in that space with girls as they grapple with their identity to write these types of college essays. I get to ask them the hard-hitting questions:

"What do you care about?"

"What do you like doing?"

"What do you want to do more of?"

This is when I sometimes find out that they've been part of the

Robotics Club in order to check an impressive box for college, but have no desire to pursue a STEM major. Instead, they want to study political science, but unfortunately not one of their extracurricular activities aligns with that interest. This situation brings girls into direct confrontation with their authentic self. And even though the situation is daunting, I continually see teenage girls courageously dive into their soul to figure out who they are and what they like.

Davina was so adamant about being her authentic self on the application that it verged on defiant. I loved it. She was going to show them who she really was, and if they didn't think she was the right fit for their school, then their loss. At least they wouldn't be rejecting a manufactured amalgamation of some girl who isn't real. One of her essays expanded on her personal motto of "Do things you're bad at."

In her sassy essay, she shared how she loves drawing but is bad at it. She took a drawing class at school, and people around her agreed that she was truly terrible. However, she still loved it. She kept doing it. She said that when she got over the need to be amazing, she recognized how much she was growing and felt emboldened by how she was honoring her passion. She liked owning her interests and skills, not letting anyone define them for her.

On Davina's college application, she did not brand herself as an artist. Yes, that was a part of her extracurriculars, but her branding came out of her authenticity to forge her own path. Do her own thing. Be her own person. She demonstrated this in all parts of her application, whether it was in her artistic pursuits or her volunteer work (where she decided to be a poll worker at the height of the pandemic during an incredibly contentious election). I doubt anyone would be surprised to hear this, but Davina got into her first-choice college. It wasn't about the boxes that she checked, but rather her commitment to her authenticity.

Davina has inspired me to boldly search my own heart and harness my own authenticity. After regularly diving into those seemingly basic college questions, I realized that I needed these questions too. I can also get so caught up in the daily grind of do, do, do and go, go, go that I'll completely lose touch with what I care about, what I like doing, and what I want to do more of.

I'm really good at organizing friends to spend time together, so I usually get pulled into the role of planner. I'll work endlessly to create fun parties, dinners, events, trips, and so much energy is expended. Only recently did I start asking myself:

Wait, do I like these people?

Did I have fun at that event?

Was the conversation at that dinner inspiring for me?

Does the intense amount of planning that went into this feel worth it?

Is there anything I'd rather be spending my time doing?

Sometimes the answers to those questions are yes and sometimes no, but the important part is that I'm asking them. I'm checking in with myself. I don't need to do something just because I'm good at it. I can make more conscious choices. How and where I invest my time will tell me A LOT about my identity.

With teenage girls, I talk about that available time and create intention in how we choose to spend it in our respective lives. They've given me ideas, perspective, and wisdom that have pushed me to listen more deeply, which brings me to the lesson I've learned from them.

*Our identity needs a lot of care to crystallize, because finding your authentic self requires listening to and trusting your inner voice, regardless of other people's expectations.*

I profoundly love helping a girl connect with her inner voice. For me, I often call this connection "listening to my heart" rather than to my brain, which can be a noisy bully of self-doubt. In order to find the framing that uniquely resonates with her, I'll ask:

"When you make a choice that feels really good to you—like you don't feel the need to question it because it feels so right in your heart—where does that inner guidance come from?"

I'll offer ideas, but girls usually respond with all sorts of helpful ways to frame it, calling it: "my intuition," "my higher self," "inner wisdom," "my soul," "in alignment," "my truth," "listening to my gut," or "listening to my heart."

Then I ask, "And how do you find ways to hear it more clearly? What helps you connect with it?"

This question inspires a variety of responses. She might say she's found it in nature, journaling, listening to music, dancing, yoga, drawing, baking, taking a bath, singing, meditating, talking with friends, praying, sitting in the sun, painting, sewing, reading, or taking a walk. These are not things I tell her to do—I look for ways she can voice them herself. There are lots of ways to frame the deepening connection with one's inner voice and authentic self. The point is to ask the right questions to get her thinking about it. Questions about her unique interests and talents will also help open up possibilities.

Sometimes, when teenage girls are grappling with the identity discovery process, I witness excessive humility pop up, which is a type of fear and hesitancy to boldly own her skills and passions. As mentioned before, self-doubt shows up in girls' worries about looking like they're bragging or demanding attention, so they'll downplay their talents and hide louder parts of their personalities.

In the same way that I like to inspire girls to own their messy "flaws," I also like to spend time encouraging them to own parts of their personalities that might seem "big." I ask her to TAKE UP SPACE.

Fourteen-year-old Viola was told a lot when she was younger that she was too loud. She tells me that now it's the reason why her identity has become quiet and shy. Her identity morphed in response to other people's commentary. I'm unclear why people are so scared of loud girls, but this type of quieting is something I hear a lot about from teenage girls, and I experienced personally.

I share with girls how I deal with it now, which is that I just call out the truth and continue being myself. Particularly when I meet someone new, I'll say early on, "Just so you know, I'm aware of how high-energy I am. I'm not putting it on, it's the real me. I genuinely have a lot of energy."

People have told me that this actually sets them at ease, thinking to themselves, "Well if she's aware of it, then it must be authentic."

This amuses me, but it's worked. Or on social media, I'll post a really bold photo that I'm excited about (most likely I'll be wearing sparkles or doing something audacious that makes me feel like my full self), and I'll include in the caption:

"This photo might be a bit much, but I'm okay with that. I can struggle with people's perception of me, but I'm going to try to use this space to always boldly be myself."

Saying that type of truth feels very liberating.

Davina, who has clearly stepped into the skill of giving zero fucks about what people think, loves when people call her "so intense" or "too much." She knows that by not having fear around her boldness, she'll help make room for other girls to be their bold self too. She's modeling and giving permission to every girl around her to *take up space*.

In downplaying their talents, I've had a lot of girls tell me that they're really good at English, so it's okay that they're not good at math. Girls often feel like they can be really good *at only one thing*.

This is when I say, "I'm really good at English and really good at math. I'm also really good at history. I know a lot about politics and I'm great at public speaking. I'm naturally good at sports, and I'm a good dancer. I'm really good at hosting parties and creating community with my friends. I'm good at getting people to volunteer for causes and teaching people about different social issues. I'm really good at chemistry and environmental science . . ."

I continue until it's reeeaaaallllly uncomfortable. A part of me still feels very uncomfortable detailing those things, but I'm trying to model the radical choice of liking myself and owning my talents. (That said, I'm still sitting here wondering if I should erase all of that because it feels so uncomfortable.)

Teenage girls are usually astounded that I can say all of that. There's a tension that builds as I keep listing things, and it's clear that I'm breaking some colossal societal rule that women should be *humble, modest,* and *self-deprecating*, which apparently has come to mean that women are not allowed to say good things about themselves.

However, if we only feel comfortable talking about the *one thing* we're allowed to be really good at, that certainly limits a lot of identity exploration. It keeps women small and quiet.

After sharing this with girls, I ask them to start listing more things they're good at. I wish everyone could watch the transformation that ensues. As they start listing more things, their painful discomfort with the activity slowly morphs into a smile that conveys, *Wow, I'm pretty cool.* Their whole body and posture shifts in response to them liking their expanding identity.

I particularly love to do this activity when they're struggling with imposter syndrome, which is the belief that "one's successes are the product of luck or fraud rather than skill."[2] I have witnessed girls really struggle with this, and research reveals how it can follow them into adulthood, as a KPMG study found that 75 percent of female executives experience imposter syndrome in their careers.[3] I've found that when a girl voices her skills and achievements out loud, she can internalize a deeper ownership over them.

I've swung to both extremes now:

Allowing space to do things you're bad at.

And allowing space to be really good at a lot of things.

*More space is what teenage girls need.*

*Space to explore who they are.*

Space to explore their identities beyond perfectionism, likability, productivity, and the rules and constraints that the world has put on them for simply identifying as a girl. This exploration can also help them discover their own unique sense of "cool."

The world has a lot of bullies telling girls what's "cool," delineating who and what they should be. Bullying can have a significant impact on a teenage girl's life, often creating wounds that last into adulthood. Sometimes when women get triggered by other women, they age-regress to a teenage girl, tapping in to the insecurities that were bullied into them. With her offbeat interests, Giselle has never felt like she fit in at school. She candidly expressed to me that bullying at school has a huge impact on identity, and it can be as simple as:

"Someone can be made fun of for the way they dress, so then they'll dress another way in order to not get bullied. Then they lose their sense of self, and they're stuck like that, until they deal with it."

I've certainly been trying to take Giselle's advice to "deal with it." Confronting a bully's narrative about me and reclaiming my own story has been very healing.

Also, not just a bully's comments, but anyone's mean comments on clothes hit *way harder* than people realize. Girls told me repeatedly for this chapter that fashion reflects identity and that it's a vital space for exploration. Learning from what girls have told me over and over again, I've come to my own conclusion that a girl desperately needs to wear whatever she wants. If you have tension around this, then I recommend having a nonjudgmental conversation about it with her, seeking to understand her clothing choices. A good starting point is:

"How does this outfit make you feel?" To keep the conversation expanding, it's good to respond with "That's cool," or "That's interesting, I hadn't thought of it like that." And then, "Why do you want to feel that?"

A tone of judgment or even seemingly light commentary on a girl's outfit will definitely spark resistance and shame. Shame particularly thrives in clothing choices. You might not like what she's wearing, but that's about you, not her. What is she needing to explore? By understanding her answers first, rather than going straight to a rule, it will help her feel heard.

Madelyn tells me, "It's empowering to feel good in what you're wearing. It's not for other people. I'm a little art project each day. It's connected to the undoing of gender, embracing both the masculine and feminine parts of myself. You feel different in what you're wearing. It changes your vibe for the day."

The more girls tell me about their clothing choices, the more I realize why a dress code for girls at school would feel like an invasion into their sense of self. This sense of self is also deeply tied to her expression of gender and sexuality.

This book would be incomplete without covering the exploration of LGBTQ+ identities that I see teenage girls stepping into these days more than ever. I know an incredibly large number of girls who identify as queer, fluid, gay, bisexual, pansexual, and other terms that they don't even want to say aloud because it feels like a box to them. I would say that "queer" is the most popular, which could mean gay, bi, or absolutely anything counter to the mainstream.

The national average age for coming out has dramatically lowered in the last few years, and it's been exciting to witness. There's not a lot of research to delineate the exact age, but some report the age is 14 years old,[4] which confirms my personal experience. I've had a lot of 14-year-old girls come out to me, sometimes before they tell their families, and it's been my absolute honor to support them. That said, I often see parents uncomfortable with the idea of their daughter expressing her sexuality in a different way than they expected.

It's interesting that adults are totally fine asking girls if they have a boyfriend or a crush starting at age six, but when a girl hits puberty, and she starts experiencing her sexual attractions in a much bigger way, people are like, "Wow, that's young."

They might be supportive, but they can't help but think she's too young to be grappling with such an identity, and that attitude rubs off on the girl whether they want it to or not. Implicit bias comes up because prior generations have considered heterosexuality the default. There is not a lot of "meeting her where she's at" because parents are often triggered by their own baggage with this topic, which activates their own agenda for dealing with this "issue." However, if by writing about this here, I can make the world safer for one queer kid to talk to their parents, then this whole book will be worth it.

It can be profoundly and terrifyingly vulnerable to share a new gender identity or sexual orientation with people, and if your natural inclination isn't to respond supportively, then another conversation outside of this book might be helpful. According to the 2023 CDC report, more than half of LGBTQ+ teenagers are experiencing ongoing extreme distress and poor mental health, with 22 percent attempting suicide in the last year.[5] And at a disproportionately higher rate, one in four Black transgender and nonbinary youth are attempting suicide.[6]

I will be focusing on much-needed, loving responses, and the Trevor Project can further provide supportive online resources, education, and guidance. In their National Survey on LGBTQ Youth Mental Health, they found that "youth who live in a community that is accepting of LGBTQ people reported significantly lower rates of attempting suicide than those who do not."[7]

When a teenage girl shares her sexual orientation with her parents, it's wildly important to give her some love, belief, trust, and also some space and ease around it. Otherwise, shame can cast its shadow. Shame is so catastrophic for teenage girls that it will have its own chapter, but it's important to note how these first memories of coming out will be kept in her heart forever. They can be filled with shame or with love. There's a choice.

I never like to make assumptions, so when we discuss romantic interests, I keep it super chill and open, not asking about a boy specifically.

"Any crushes you're into these days?"

I affirm her for however she's choosing to navigate, keeping it casual. If she wants to share more, I don't recommend asking lots of questions that try to gather data on what you want to know. Girls don't want adults to make these moments into a whole big thing, because whatever her sexual orientation might be, they don't like to feel romantic pressure from adults. She will shut you out quickly if it becomes awkward or doesn't feel safe.

To create safety and an inviting environment around sexual orientation conversations, I recommend complimenting LGBTQ+ teenagers on TV shows you both might watch at casual times when you know she'll hear, or if someone you both know comes out, then say how happy you are for them. Before ever coming out, it's so helpful for a girl to hear how you are a safe and positive supporter of the LGBTQ+ community.

If a conversation does turn into a coming-out moment, please, most importantly, meet her with clear love and affirmation. I'd want you to find your own words, but an example of a response that I've given is:

"That's so wonderful, I'm so happy for you. Thank you for telling me. It's so beautiful and cool that you're stepping into the fullness of who you are. Let me know how I can support you." It's good for parents to emphasize:

"I love you. Nothing has changed."

I use the words *love* and *loving* a lot in this section because girls have shared with me that love should definitely be verbalized, but they've also told me that responses can be more casual than you'd expect. Several girls explained this nuance to me.

"It can be casual because you don't want to feel like coming out will change anything in a major way and you also don't want to feel like you're stepping into some brand-new identity for the first time, because most girls know for quite a while before coming out."

Girls have shared that a parent can seem supportive by giving the common response "It's good to experiment," but that response has actually made girls feel like their parent didn't believe them or thought it was "a passing phase." Instead, it's best to listen closely and reflect on the words she's using.

Overall, I don't want a parent to miss out on the opportunity to create trust, respect, and *love*.

I know parents can be scared of this type of identity expression because they've seen a societal response of discrimination and violence. Many girls emphasized with me: "If parents are scared, imagine how young girls feel trying to address their fears. It is so important to always hold a safe and accepting environment from a very young age so shame and fear aren't built up."

Times are changing, and we have to decide if we're a part of that change. Living in fear only affirms the status quo. According to the U.S. Department of Education, our status quo currently shows that 40 percent of homeless youth identify as LGBTQ+.[8] These kids' stories often share the heartbreaking commonality that they felt safer living on the street than with their family who didn't accept them for who they are.

Most of the parents I know have been very accepting of their daughter's sexual orientation, but I've still had a girl cry in my arms with abject terror that her parents would kick her out of the house if she came out to them. That's not what happened when she eventually told them, but she still felt paralyzing shame around her identity because she had heard her parents make negative remarks about LGBTQ+ issues.

In my experience, shame and fear around a girl's developing identity will enormously and negatively impact her. Whereas unconditional support as she explores and embraces her authentic self has a strikingly positive effect.

Letting teenage girls be who they need to be, discover what they need to discover, and trust that they'll find a path that's right for them is about redefining our relationship with control. We can try to control their choices, which I see end in drama, pain, resentment, and disconnection. Or we can try to genuinely listen to them, which also empowers them to listen to their inner voice.

Many "successful" people throughout history have emphasized the importance of the inner voice and authenticity.

Apple founder and CEO Steve Jobs said in his Stanford commencement speech: "Don't let the noise of others' opinions drown out your own inner voice."[9]

Former first lady Michelle Obama said, "There's power in allowing yourself to be known and heard, in owning your unique story, in using your authentic voice."[10]

Foundational feminist writer and activist Betty Friedan wrote in *The Feminine Mystique*: "It is easier to live through someone else than to complete yourself. The freedom to lead and plan your own life is frightening if you have never faced it before. It is frightening when a woman finally realizes that there is no answer to the question 'Who am I?' except the voice inside herself."[11]

Answering the question "Who am I?" is a life endeavor that no one should be invading or impeding. There is only one person who can determine if a girl is aligned with her authenticity. She can. No one else can answer that for her. So, with love, trust, and acceptance, how about we all just give her some space to figure it out.

Parents really need to let girls make their own choices about things that express their identity—clothes, activities, decorating their room—because it helps them discover who they are. I used to feel covered up, like no one could see me, but now I've made it my purpose to explore who I am, and I've become more confident and happy with each new discovery.

—WAVERLY, AGE 15

+ Our identity needs a lot of care to crystallize, because finding your authentic self requires listening to and trusting your inner voice, regardless of other people's expectations.

+ Our identity often forms from receiving attention for things we're good at, but we also need to reflect and ask if we even like that identity.

+ We need to encourage girls and women to take up space and be unapologetically themselves.

+ Create space to explore your identity by doing things you're bad at, without any obligation to productivity or achievement.

+ It's crucial to create a safe, inviting, and loving environment for teenage girls to share all parts of their identity.

## CHAPTER THIRTEEN

# SHAME

*We're only as sick as our secrets.*[1]
—adage from 12-step recovery programs

Shame seeps into every aspect of our lives, like carbon monoxide poisoning: odorless, tasteless, invisible to the eye, unknowingly infiltrating the air we breathe . . . until it kills us.

As expert shame researcher Brené Brown defines it: "Shame is the most powerful, master emotion. It's the fear that we're not good enough."

There are so many complexities around the topic of shame, and Brown is a great resource to explore further, but I'm here to present the pervasive truth that shame invades every topic of this book. I've learned more about shame working with teenage girls than I'd ever want to.

Shame seeping in from parents when they tell their daughter, "Are you insane? You're not leaving the house wearing that. You look like a tramp."

Shame seeping into a girl's relationship with a boy when she tells me, "I feel ashamed if I don't put his needs first. And if I don't please him, then I feel even worse."

Shame seeping into her sense of identity: "Having immigrant parents, I always feel out of place. At school, I'm too Mexican, and at home I'm too white-washed. I'm never enough."

Shame seeping into her body as she proclaims, "I'm too fat to go to prom."

Shame seeping into her goals as I hear: "If I don't get into an Ivy League college, my dad won't love me."

Shame seeping into her trauma, even when she's fighting so hard to heal: "I know the rape wasn't my fault, but maybe, I don't know, maybe I could have done something different."

Shame seeping into her relationship with money: "She rolled her eyes that I couldn't buy the concert ticket, but her parents are paying for it. I have to work an after-school job to afford even the small stuff."

Shame seeping into her menstruation struggles: "I was really far from my house when I started my period, so I had to stop at a store and realized I had no cash to buy tampons. I was just looking at the cashier, helplessly bleeding, humiliated."

Shame seeping in through racism when a Black student tells me, "They accused me of stealing at the Rite Aid. They treated me like a criminal, and I felt like shit."

On a weekly basis, there are countless examples of upsetting, shame-filled stories that girls share with me. Consequently, I've needed to learn how to show up for these girls in the darkest of times, which means increasing my understanding around shame.

From 18-year-old Harper's witty jokes and playful spirit, one might not guess the large amount of shame she's constantly battling on a daily basis, but thankfully, she's invited me into that heavy space in the hopes of supporting her. She tells me, "Shame is a very body-oriented, sexually oriented experience for young women. Whether it's the soul-crushing pressure to be thin, the purity culture, the never-ending slut-shaming, or the silencing rape culture, shame is so inescapable that it's normalized."

She sadly references the same old story, a girl's body and her sexuality. I've covered body image a lot in this book, but when the term "body shame" is specifically used in research, 94 percent of teenage girls report having experienced body shame.[2]

When I asked girls for their thoughts on the chapter covering sexuality, every single one of them told me that I needed to address slut-shaming. A nationally representative 2011 survey found that slut-shaming is one of the most common forms of sexual harassment that teenage girls face,[3] and with the advent of social media, I would argue that it's gotten worse. According to the National Institutes of Health, 80 percent of girls have witnessed the use of "slut" as an insult online.[4]

Fifteen-year-old Rosy tells me, "I've seen girls being called a slut when they do a lot of makeup or just talk to a lot of dudes. A guy at my school can wear his jeans so low that it shows his boxers, *his underwear*, and no one cares, but if a girl wears short shorts, she's called a whore by kids and gets a dress code violation."

I'd like to point out that "slut-shaming" is not a term teenage girls invented. It's the product of the system that surrounds them (that adults actively participate in) and a society that viciously devours a teenage girl's sexuality with a ravenous appetite for fear. Cal State Long Beach professor Shira Tarrant, who researches gender and sexuality politics, aptly notes, "We don't even have a word to describe a happy, joyous, sexually active female." The primary word being used has *shame* built into it. Tarrant calls it gendered or sexualized bullying with long-term consequences that include depression, self-hatred, alienation, suicide, sexual fear, and sexual recklessness.[5]

That's heavy. I'll lean into this intensity, but I think it's important to take a step back and look at some seemingly subtler ways that shame shows up for girls. These larger issues can feel overwhelming, so I want to start in a simpler place. I see the seeds of shame take root early on, and it can be as basic as how well a girl is doing with multiplication facts.

Particularly with education, I've learned that when I'm trying to teach an academic concept, and I sense there's shame behind the girl's process, I'm not going to make any progress until that root shame is addressed. Multiplication facts are a very common example of how this plays out. I'll be working with a 16-year-old who I discover has been hiding the reality that she doesn't know her multiplication facts. She knows that they were supposed to be mastered in fourth grade, but somehow, she's been able to glide by just enough to not let anyone know her struggle. She's been hiding this secret that many girls have revealed to me as "Yeah, I'm secretly dumb."

When they say this, sometimes their body hunches over, letting the shame take hold as a state of broken embarrassment, sometimes they put up a tough front of "it's stupid, it doesn't matter," and sometimes they shrug their shoulders with a defeated apathy that has been stealthily destroying their education.

Of course, I don't think they're actually dumb, *not in the slightest.* I know it seems like a heavy reaction to some multiplication facts, but I've found it to be so commonplace that I've started calling it their "math trauma."

Instead of diving into memorizing multiplication facts right away, I spend some time getting to know their math trauma. I ask her, "Is there a teacher in the past who shamed you for your math ability?"

I've found that there's always a clear person, and girls vividly recount how much that shame took root in their identity, usually around age seven or eight. They feel like it was a moment that defined their intelligence and potential. For years, these girls have been trying to hide from this scary idea that they might not be smart, and consequently, it has blocked them from so much of the learning process.

Sitting in these types of shame-filled spaces way too many times, I've learned from my time with teenage girls that *shame is profoundly disempowering, as it toxically blocks deep human connection and our potential to grow.*

I've found that there's an easy way to identify shame—just think of anything that you're afraid to talk about. Feeling embarrassed is also usually a good clue to look for. It's often a portal to a deeper shame that's been hiding and festering, possibly consciously or unconsciously.

Unfortunately, I also witness shame being used as a tool to try to teach or "protect" teenage girls. I've seen a mom tell her daughter that her outfit is too slutty, thinking that will make her change clothes, which will then help protect her from the threatening attention from boys. Teenage girls are smart enough to see this game being played, but shame coming from parents is particularly poisonous. Over FaceTime, 17-year-old Izzy's face turns sullen when I bring up shame. She grievously tells me:

"Grown-ups use shame to try to help us realize our mistakes, but instead that shame hits us much deeper, and it stays. Parents are trying to use shame as a tool to their advantage to make us do what they want, what they think is right . . . but it backfires and hurts us. When we feel terrible about ourselves, we don't make good choices."

A lot of that shame is shoved into the dark, hiding deep within her. However, I see clues that it's there when she's afraid to talk about things like her body, her sexuality, academics that she's not understanding, something she can't afford to buy, racial comments at school, or the pressures she feels from her family. These topics are messier, not black and white, and without clear answers, so we have to sit in the discomfort of imperfection. We're back to "embracing the gray." With care and clear intentions of not being judgmental, I join her in the mess.

In the effort to create emotional safety around this space of gray, I try to teach girls the art of "Both/And." It's a psychology tool that "says that you can and almost certainly will feel more than one thing at a time," which "creates breathing room so you can work through an experience without judgment."[6] For example, a girl can love her family AND feel like her family shames her for not being smart enough. It can be Both. A girl can like the way she looks in a dress AND feel frustrated that she doesn't look like the model on the billboard. It can be Both. She doesn't have to hate her body just because she doesn't look like the model. This shift gives them just enough room for a little light to shine on the covert shame that I find hidden beneath so much binary thinking.

To lean into the psychology conversation more with a teenage girl, I often discuss the research of Stanford University psychologist Carol Dweck's fixed mindset vs. growth mindset, which can be defined as:

"Someone with a *growth mindset* views intelligence, abilities, and talents as learnable and capable of improvement through effort. On the other hand, someone with a *fixed mindset* views those same traits as inherently stable and unchangeable over time."[7]

I'm bringing up psychology concepts here because I've found they captivate a teenage girl's interest and intellectual capability. I've never met a teenage girl who doesn't love to talk about psychology. Dweck's "growth mindset" is one of those topics that continually enthralls them. One of my students first read about it in middle school, and it impacted her so intensely that she referenced it in her college application essay five years later.

The concept gives girls hope that their reality isn't *forever.* They aren't *fixed,* and they are always capable of *growth.* Without that little bit of hope, shame becomes the all-consuming venom that seeps into the blood, convincing her that nothing is ever going to change.

With each new generation, I've witnessed a passion for mental health blossom, and within the isolation of the COVID-19 pandemic, I saw a teenage girl's enthusiasm for therapy *explode.* Over the last few years, more than ever, I've had girls ask me for the contact info for potential therapists or helped girls whose families can't afford those therapists find support groups or free counseling services in their community. A teenage girl feels empowered by the idea of understanding how her brain works. Embracing the conversation, I've witnessed 16-year-olds healing trauma and familial wounds so much earlier than my friends who didn't really start unloading their decades of baggage in therapy until their thirties and forties. Personally, I know that so much of that baggage centers around shame.

I had a very hard time accessing my hidden shame until I walked into a 12-step Al-Anon recovery room in my thirties, which focuses on supporting people who have a friend or family member whose drinking is impacting their lives. Thankfully, 12-step recovery groups deeply understand the need to shine light on our secrets. Not only does their adage "We're only as sick as our secrets" name the problem, but they also provide a solution. Sharing. The act of sharing my secrets and shame at Al-Anon meetings is one of the most revolutionary and healing acts I've experienced in my life. Everyone there listens, without commentary, and they listen with so much empathy, because they've been in those dark places too.

Brené Brown has found a lot of evidence to support this phenomenon in her research, as she describes:

"Shame derives its power from being unspeakable."[8]

AND . . .

"If we can share our story with someone who responds with empathy and understanding, shame can't survive."[9]

Sharing that there was alcoholism in my family, a secret that unearthed so much shame for me, in a room full of empathy, understanding, and care, allowed me to unburden myself. I was able to set my shame free, so that it was no longer lingering and hiding inside me.

For teenage girls, shame around sexual assault is the largest villain I've come up against. A girl is usually shamed into silence and destructive pain because she's terrified no one will believe her.

In her freshman year of college, Harper was raped by a guy she was dating, and she tells me, "Shame was the sole motivator for the silence around my rape. The culture of victim-blaming told me that it was my fault. I felt ashamed of my choices even though it was someone else's choice to violate me." It was important to Harper that she share her story here, because she offers this hope:

"The more we talk about sexual assault, the less stigmatized it'll become, and the less shame girls will feel."

Tragically, I know many other teenage girls who could share a similar story.

That's why the #MeToo movement was so revelatory and liberating. So many women have faced some type of sexual violence, whether it's physical, emotional, or verbal, and it usually has the same effect: shame. By women and girls proclaiming "Me Too" across the world, sharing their pain, we discovered that we're not alone. The founder of #MeToo, Tarana Burke, so aptly summarizes the impact of the movement when she says, "'Me Too' is about using the power of empathy to stomp out shame."[10]

I've learned that when I don't feel alone in my pain, I have more courage. The fear has less power over me because the burden feels lighter. The consequences of remaining in that state of fear and shame cannot be overstated. Fear and shame will guide someone down a path of addiction, violence, behavioral disorders, anxiety, bullying, hopelessness, and self-destruction.

If you want to create a safe space for a teenage girl to talk about shame, I recommend using a lot of the techniques that have been discussed so far in this book. First and foremost, please don't underestimate a teenage girl's ability to engage in deep conversations and self-reflection.

This process of sharing our shame in a loving space brings together all the lessons I've addressed, and I can guide you into that process using each of the chapter titles we've covered so far.

I've needed to invite teenage girls into conversations, many of which start by simply questioning *The Media* around us. I ask questions that spark her thoughts on difficult topics. I welcome her *Choice* if she wants to share her struggles with me, while I vulnerably share how I struggle and can empathize with difficult topics like *Sexuality* and *Beauty*. I've needed to assure her that I'm supporting her with the devotion of a *Friend* who loves her, even in the mess. I've needed to create distance from the harmful habits of *Perfection*, *People-Pleasing*, and *Self-Doubt* so as to create a safe space that allows her authentic *Identity* to be shared with *Radical Honesty*. I ask each question with genuine care, and I prepare to hold space for some big *Feelings* without trying to "fix" her.

And then I fucking listen. Deeply listen. And when *Shame* finds its way out of hiding, it's critical that I let her feel all the feelings. When it seems like she's expressed herself fully, I ask, "Is there anything else you want to share? I love hearing what you have to say."

And when she's done, I acknowledge her feelings, empathize, and then I *Compliment* her. I try to compliment her in a way that acknowledges her feelings, celebrates her uniqueness, and helps her feel understood because I'm reflecting back the exact words she used without any solution, advice, or forced positivity. The simple act of sharing is enough—more than enough. It's revolutionary.

Teenage girls tell me that adults never deeply listen to them. I would venture to say that adults rarely deeply listen to each other. Deeply listening demands presence, nonjudgment, generosity, and an overall sensitivity for the feelings *beneath* the words. When we're lovingly present, we can often experience a deeper, emotional layer of meaning beyond the words being used. As critical as it is to share our secrets and pain with each other, it's equally critical to listen, because that space creates emotional safety.

Listening with empathy and compassion is ideal, but I think we could really start back at the basics. People have gotten really bad at listening. While another person talks, we're usually spending that time thinking of what we're going to say next. Listening and then responding with empathy is particularly important when it's a heavier topic filled with shame. And thankfully, it's a lot simpler. Empathy reflects the exact words that a girl says and replies with genuine care:

"That's awful," "I'm so sorry that happened," "Of course you feel angry," "It makes sense you feel that way," "Yeah, that's really hard."

This empathetic space can open hearts in a way that brings real, meaningful connection.

If there weren't enough sources of shame already for teenage girls to manage, I've witnessed another layer of shame. Society and adults have created a cliché of fear around teenage girls that stereotypes them as superficial, overly emotional, dumb, mean, and irrational. All those stigmas, on top of the very real shame she encounters, create quite the cesspool of feeling awful about herself. And worst of all, this destroys her innate, dazzling, dynamic power.

When a culture of shame digs its sharp, vicious teeth into a girl's sense of identity, it blocks her personal connection to her power, which is what helps her pursue greater possibilities in life. Whereas liberation from shame unleashes a very exciting type of power, a power that's worthy of our final exploration in this book because the space of empowerment is how we create change.

We underestimate how much power we can give back to a teenage girl just by simply listening to her story. I'm so grateful to have found people in my life willing to listen to my inner teenager's story, so that she could find some healing and take back her power. I want you to find those trusted people in your life and share your secrets with them. Because the truth is, all of our stories are full of shame, and that makes us human.

Our messy humanness is where we can experience the deepest and most loving connections to others and to ourselves. Shame tries to keep us small and separate. However, sharing and listening expands our walls to include people who then can offer love. It's the type of love that feels really genuine because that person knows our brokenness and is still loving us. We don't have to hide behind walls. And even better, teenage girls can help us envision a world without shame that doesn't need walls in the first place.

**CORE INSIGHTS**

Growing up, I carried a lot of shame. As many girls do. It was almost like a part of my identity and I often found myself slipping through the never-ending sinkhole of shame. I felt like I wasn't allowed to take up space—or was undeserving of it—so I tried to make myself small. Now, as a 19-year-old, I allow myself to take up space— physically, mentally, and emotionally.

Now, I feel like I have the opportunity to be my full self while maintaining the ability to grow. —CAMILA, AGE 19

---

+ Shame infiltrates every topic of this book, but it's sneaky, and can be identified by thinking about anything you're afraid or embarrassed to talk about.

+ Shame is disempowering, as it toxically blocks human connection and our potential to grow.

+ Incorporating a growth mindset and a Both/And approach can interrupt shame-filled patterns to allow space for adopting new, healthier perspectives.

- ✦ The consequences of remaining in a state of hidden fear can be severe, but sharing your shame with people who respond with empathy can create profound healing.

- ✦ Teenage girls will share and process shame if emotional safety is created through nonjudgmental, compassionate listening.

## CHAPTER FOURTEEN

# POWER

*Girls are one of the most powerful forces for change in the world:*
*When their rights are recognized, their needs are met,*
*and their voices are heard, they drive positive change in*
*their families, their communities, and the world.*[1]
—Kathy Calvin
(former United Nations Foundation president & CEO)

Over the years, I've supported many teenage girls' election campaigns to become their school's student body president, which invariably means that I hear, "What if I don't win? What if I'm not the best choice to be president?"

In this book, I've certainly scrutinized how society/parents/adults all limit a teenage girl's power. But it's also important to note that teenage girls can limit their own power. Their fear stems from the issues I've already covered, but more importantly, I want to highlight how a girl is taught a very limiting concept of leadership and power.

This conversation won't be an analysis of the many academic suppositions on what power is and isn't. Instead, I'm going to share the perspective of a very diverse group of teenage girls, and what they think about the world of power we've built around them. Quite simply, teenage girls aren't inspired by the spaces that have been traditionally characterized as "powerful."

They don't always see themselves winning the school presidency because mainstream leadership roles haven't always represented their value system, which will be expanded upon in this chapter. The models of power that surround us don't resonate for her as a healthy solution to the world's problems. For so long, power has been particularly related to domination and self-interest.

Davina was quick to point out, "Women don't take advantage of power in the same way men do, which is why TV shows are made about women like Elizabeth Holmes." (Holmes cheated people out of millions of dollars while for years she lied about the technical capabilities of her company, Theranos, a blood-testing firm, resulting in a hit Hulu TV show about her.)

Davina remarks: "I think TV shows made about men lying and defrauding people are boring, because they're obvious, I'm not surprised. But a woman doing that? That's rare and therefore entertaining. It's awful, and not what I want in this world, but there's a reason it's so addictive to watch."

With her astute observations, Davina is bringing light to an issue that comes up a lot for teenage girls: *Women trying to model men in power, which they believe has left women very unsatisfied with their options.* Girls also share how exhausting it is because they're trying to be something they're not, something that goes against their natural way of being.

When I was recently having lunch with Izzy, I asked for her first thoughts on power. She quickly responded, "I think instantly of authority. I never think that I have authority, and I always think of someone having authority over me."

My heart sank, and I asked her what she thinks the solution is. She said wisely, "Oh, everything needs to change, the whole system. We need to redefine power."

I smiled. This is my favorite type of conversation. I would love nothing more than for all of us to rethink the whole system. . . .

In psychological science, power is defined as "one's capacity to alter another person's condition or state of mind by providing or withholding resources—such as food, money, knowledge, and affection—or administering punishments, such as physical harm, job termination, or social ostracism."[2] So yes, that's certainly not a definition where I'm like, "Yay, cool, sounds good!" Instead, I'm going to stand alongside Izzy and explore how we can do it all differently.

Basically, domination has been the name of the game for so long. The United States seems to have power because of its military and economic domination in the world. And historically, there's a great deal of systemic oppression that has stemmed from efforts to maintain power. American scholar and author bell hooks (who purposely kept her pen name lowercase in order to keep the focus on her work rather than herself) describes this dark side of American culture with a necessary bluntness:

"In an imperialist racist patriarchal society that supports and condones oppression, it is not surprising that men and women judge their worth, their personal power, by their ability to oppress others."[3]

Alongside domination, teenage girls often view power as the same thing as oppression, because historically the concepts have gone hand in hand. I cannot address the idea of power without acknowledging that critical intersectional lens of oppression, which sheds light on how people of different races, genders, abilities, socioeconomic status, nationalities, religions, and sexual orientations can face multiple, overlapping, interconnected types of discrimination. These systemic disadvantages continue to affect a person's political, social, and economic power in the world and require much-needed justice.

For this conversation, the primary oppressive commonality for teenage girls is their gender identity as women, which will be a point of focus. In extended discussions covering oppression, intersectionality is always crucial and would illuminate examples of how transgender girls experience more discrimination than cisgender girls and BIPOC girls experience racial prejudice that white girls don't experience.

In respect to our focus here on women and girls' gender identity,

I've found that people really don't know how recently women of all races gained some seemingly obvious rights. Most people don't know that women weren't allowed to have their own credit card until 1974, become an astronaut until 1978, or run in the Boston Marathon until 1972. Historically, men have had more rights, and those rights have given them a certain type of power.

In addition to domination and oppression, money is a topic that must be included in conversations on power. I don't need to state the obvious facts on how money has been connected to power throughout history, but I'd like to point out how money has always been a part of the women's liberation conversation. Women being prevented from working, not affording childcare, suffering from the pay gap, marrying for financial security, or staying in bad marriages because of money have all been a part of the historical conversation. I'm not saying that earning wealth is the goal here, I'm saying that financial access, competency, stability, and independence have created a viable path for women to find their own power.

I'm incredibly passionate about teaching teenage girls financial literacy, and when they kept asking me for more info, I ended up creating a summer curriculum for them because nowhere else in their education were finances being addressed. Girls love learning about it so much that they're willing to give up free time in the summer to sit on Zoom with me to learn about money—how to make it, save it, and invest it. Many of them have told me how annoyed they are that "Money is such a boys' club!"

I'll go over budgeting, investing, building credit, and types of bank accounts with them, and then my favorite thing to do is help them open an account. I do this with girls who have drastically different family incomes, and whether the amount of money going into the account is big or small, the effect is the same. It's empowering for a girl or woman of any age to have her own bank account.

I opened my first bank account at 11, which defined my relationship with money early on. I earned some money dog-sitting, and my dad walked me to the local bank to open my first savings account. It was this really positive, bonding experience with my dad that made me love the idea of saving money to this day. He taught me about getting higher interest rates, and I was putting money into CDs by the time I was 12. Additionally, my mom gave me a clothing budget around that age, allowing me to buy whatever I wanted within that small monthly amount. I would often save up for months at a time, intricately planning how I was going to execute my spending choices. It was early engagement like this that helped me understand the power of money.

More importantly, I felt powerful knowing about money. I felt powerful being responsible with it. And I felt respected by my parents because they were trusting me with something that was clearly important to the world.

Respect is something so important to a teenage girl. I've been emphasizing it throughout this book: how we can better respect a girl's thoughts, feelings, choices, and identity. As Davina asserts:

"If I could make it the way I want, power would be about respect."

When I ask her, "What do you think holds women back from getting that respect, that power?" She thinks about it and then scrunches her face.

"You know, it's so normal for women not to have power, that it feels weird and uncomfortable to even want it."

I've personally encountered this struggle because the prominent narratives of power are not something I've wanted. Not only does power often signify domination, oppression, and self-interest, but women and girls are particularly excluded when physical power is respected and prioritized. I'm not inspired by it, and like Davina, it feels weird to want it. I actually believe that power's dominant narratives don't leave men feeling good either. Liz Plank's *For the Love of Men: A New Vision for Mindful Masculinity*[4] lovingly analyzes how our societal constructs of masculine power can hurt men just as much as they hurt women, which is a topic worthy of its own examination with an intersectional lens. Instead of being mad at men and society, I've had to search for myself and discover a different type of power, one that comes from within.

In highlighting that choice for women, bell hooks illuminates, "If any female feels she need anything beyond herself to legitimate and validate her existence, she is already giving away her power to be self-defining, her agency."[5]

There are so many oppressive narratives swirling around me at any time that it can be easy to accidentally give away my power and agency to define myself. But with Gen Z in particular, I've witnessed a deep need to own their unique self and advocate for a more expansive existence. These girls grew up watching *The Hunger Games* and *Moana*, not *Sleeping Beauty*. They want change, they want to be leaders, and we shouldn't be underestimating their vision for the future.

However, I'm genuinely wondering when the world is going to catch up to them. According to the UN, as of January 1, 2023, there are only 31 countries where women are serving as heads of state and/or government. At this rate, gender equality in the highest positions of power won't be achieved for another hundred and thirty years.[6]

THIS ISN'T GOOD ENOUGH.

It's facts like these that make teenage girls want to scream.

In business leadership, it's just as bad. At the beginning of 2023, there was this big celebration that just over 10 percent of Fortune 500 companies are now run by women,[7] the most ever. . . .

Yay??

Cue: My head falling into my hands with hopeless frustration. I'm *so very tired* of celebrating itty-bitty progress for women functioning within our traditional models of power. And out of the 500 CEOs, only three of them are women of color, all during an era that's considered "progress."

It makes sense that Davina feels uncomfortable about wanting power because she doesn't like what it currently looks like.

And in addition to the lack of opportunity, the journey of pursuing these leadership accomplishments is also incredibly taxing on girls. When they have big goals, I often see them turn to perfectionist habits in an attempt to fulfill that vision. The teenage girl, her parents, her teachers, and the world around her all push for perfect grades and behavior, with everyone jumping into the Never-Ending Stress Box of productivity and academic achievement. To fit into that box, I often see her galloping spirit muzzled because that box can be quite small.

Women's power is something new and not comfortably manipulated to fit into the old, traditional models. Education is crucial, but I've found that grades are not the best indicator of a girl's potential power. So much of her power simply begins with her voice. Not only helping her find her voice but also letting her speak.

My approach in finding and encouraging a girl's voice is to ask her: "What do you care about?"

This taps into her superpower—her feelings.

When she connects to her feelings and starts speaking out loud the things she cares about, she starts discovering her values. It's then absolutely critical that I LISTEN. I listen closely until I realize another question that might prompt her deeper into her ideas and beliefs.

"What type of unfairness makes you sad or angry?"

"How could you help or change that?"

"What do you think the solution is?"

And then I listen deeply for what type of encouragement or support she might need. I meet her exactly where she's at without forcing anything.

During an exchange like this, I've actually had one conversation come up a lot more than others. Many girls tell me that they care about their family. Then they share their heavy distress that their dad disapproves of "feminism." Of course, it's not all fathers, but unfortunately with the fathers who disapprove, I'm never surprised by their timeworn criticisms: "Feminism is for angry women," "There's no point to it," "It's man-hating!"

I used to be weighed down by these words, feeling helpless. But over the years, I've learned a new way to empower a girl to respond with her voice. I start by teaching her the actual definition of *feminism*, which the *Cambridge Dictionary* defines as:

"The belief that women should be allowed the same rights, power, and opportunities as men."[8]

Then she practices saying it out loud. She practices identifying herself as a feminist, while at the same time defining it. I'll even role-play a new exchange, deepening my voice and taking on a gruff attitude, which helps activate her strength:

**Me (playing her father):** Feminism wants to hurt men!

**Teenage Girl:** I'm a feminist, Dad, which by definition means that I believe women should be allowed the same rights, power, and opportunities as men. Do you not believe in that?

**Me (playing her father):** That's not the way feminism seems to me.

**Teenage Girl:** Okay, but that's actually what it means. So, I'm going to make my choice based on the *Cambridge Dictionary* definition. With that meaning, I'm proud to be a feminist. I would hope that you would want me to have the same rights and opportunities as you.

Then, I tell her that she can exit the conversation if she wants. She doesn't need to prove herself. She can make her own choice, be her own person, step into her own power. She can voice her beliefs and values without needing a man to agree with them.

After trying this with their dads, teenage girls usually excitedly report back to me with one of these two responses:

"It went so well! He agreed with that definition and now he calls himself a feminist!!"

Or:

"It went so well! I said my truth. I stood by my beliefs, and I didn't even care if my dad agreed with me!!"

Giving a voice to her power usually involves a feeling of liberation. In this scenario, a daughter is liberating herself from her father's opinion. She finds herself free to make her own choices about her beliefs, which is so empowering. This process is closely tied with "breaking rules" and cutting the metal chain of "shoulds" wrapped around her neck. It's a process that helps her stop caring about what other people think. It's a practice that's easier said than done, but as writer and social scientist Mohadesa Najumi aptly notes:

"The woman who does not require validation from anyone is the most feared individual on the planet."[9]

This individual is empowered and liberated from the systems that have tried to contain and define her. But why is she feared? Because she can't be controlled and dominated? Or because people fear what they do not know? There are still so many unknowns around what a world of fully liberated and powerful women and girls would look like.

This brings me back to Izzy, who is saying that we should redefine *power*. Yes, I agree, and what does that look like?

My approach is going to be a gendered oversimplification, but unfortunately, sometimes, I can't perfectly address the world's complexity when I'm hunting for ways into these conversations with girls. Considering men have predominantly held positions of leadership, power has been historically characterized as masculine. I've found it helpful to initiate conversations with teenage girls on what feminine models of power might look like. I've found that the conversation truly lights them up from within. The easiest starting point has been to ask teenage girls what they think *a world with a majority of women leaders* would look like, and I can't wait for you to hear their perspective.

Izzy shared, "Less war. Women don't bottle their anger. We express our emotions. When men don't express emotions, it comes out as violence instead. Women express their feelings, communicate, and move on, without violence."

Olivia told me, "The world would be so much more equal, more fair, and everyone would be heard more."

Davina declared, "Women lead with less ego and more care, which leads to harm reduction."

Waverly said, "Women can get to the heart of what makes things unfair. Women deal with a lot, so they have more empathy for people's struggles. Since they're so in touch with their emotions, they ask a lot of 'why' questions. Instead of just throwing someone in jail, women would ask, 'Why do you think someone stole the bread? Were they not able to afford food? Let's fix why they had to steal in the first place.'"

Peeta told me, "Having women be the world's business leaders would put more focus on care. There would be more care for the customers, care for the product, care for the employees, and care for the environmental and social impact on the world."

Harper shared, "The world would be kinder. I think toxic masculinity directly translates into war. A world run by women is one rooted in cooperation instead of violence."

Jade said, "More peaceful, less violent, more communication . . . I mean, no hate to men, but women just communicate better. We'd all feel more listened to."

Lauryn told me, "I think the world would function a lot more positively. We'd be a lot more optimistic and joyful."

Yes. Yes. Yes. Yes.

These responses give us such insight on the type of change to our power structures that teenage girls need and want. So how can we make this happen?

I can tell you that when teenage girls are empowered to identify their values and act on them, they can transform the world. I've personally witnessed awe-inspiring endeavors over the years. A 14-year-old started a nonprofit that makes pillows to comfort little kids at the local children's hospital. A 15-year-old pushed her school's administration until they included more BIPOC authors in their required literature. A 16-year-old fundraised over $2,000 to support a sex education program for underserved public schools. A 17-year-old organized and led her entire school in a student walkout to protest gun violence. A 16-year-old filmed and edited a short film on teenagers' mental health during the COVID-19 pandemic. A 17-year-old organized a large cohort of voters, postcarders, phone bankers, text bankers, and poll workers for the 2020 election. The list could go on and on.

These triumphs didn't stem from good grades. Each girl actualized these meaningful accomplishments out of her genuine care and the courage to use her voice. When 16-year-old Cynthia organized an event for a nonprofit working to end gender-based violence, she planned to give a speech to the two hundred attendees. She was so nervous about it that she could barely function, and I thought she was going to have a panic attack. But when the moment came, she stepped into her power and brought the crowd to tears. She told me afterward that she was motivated by the thought "Maybe my words will matter. Maybe my voice will make a difference."

That's what gave her courage. She wasn't aiming to dominate others or show her power. Her power was a natural effect from activating her care and courage.

This brings me to the greatest lesson I've learned from the wisdom of teenage girls. Something that permeates every lesson in this book. I've learned that the forces of care and courage combine to create an even greater force that teenage girls infuse into everything they do. I've learned that *love is the most powerful force on the planet. The most powerful way to create something new and better in this world is through love.*

Maybe that sounds cheesy to you, but I hope not. Most people know this truth about love, whether overtly or buried deep in their soul. I know that I'm not saying anything new. However, I don't think we're at the point yet where society's conversations around power are integrated with discussions of love. Author adrienne maree brown (who also prefers her name spelled with lowercase letters) frames it beautifully when she says:

"If the goal was to increase the love, rather than winning or dominating a constant opponent, I think we could actually imagine liberation from constant oppression. We would suddenly be seeing everything we do, everyone we meet, not through the tactical eyes of war, but through eyes of love. We would see that there's no such thing as a blank canvas, an empty land or a new idea—but everywhere there is complex, ancient, fertile ground full of potential."[10]

That powerful potential is so expansive because love is so expansive.

My experiences with teenage girls have been filled with *so much love.* That said, I'm not sure people think of love when they first think of teenage girls. Teenage girls themselves might not label their power as a force of love because it shows up in more specific words, like the ones they mentioned in connection to women's leadership: "care," "equal," "communication," "empathy," "less ego," "peaceful," "optimistic," "listening," "kindness," "fair," "cooperation," "joyful."

But what about all that angst? I haven't forgotten it. Jade made sure to remind me to not underestimate the power of a teenage girl's angst, expressing how her desire to be listened to, her rage, her feelings, all fuel her power. This is when I asked Jade, "Is there any way the angst is connected to love?" Jade thought about it for a while and then smiled to herself. I shared her words at the beginning of this book, and now they resonate more deeply for me:·

"The angst is coming from things not sitting right in my heart. It's not that I want to create a world with more angst. Teenage girls have this fighting spirit because we can so clearly see what's broken."

It's not sitting right *in her heart.*

When I asked Izzy what it feels like to step into her power, she described it as:

"I know it in my heart first. And then that connects to my voice, so I can start speaking it."

It starts in her heart.

Teenage girls have the type of love in their heart that comes with three exclamation points. Whether it's talking about Harry Styles, commenting on an Instagram post, or texting me on my birthday, I can count on a plethora of emojis and !!! The enthusiasm makes me feel really loved. These are not people-pleasing exclamation points—they are used when they're celebrating, supporting, encouraging, and lifting up those around them. I see adults shrug off this type of exclamation-point-love as immature, superficial, and silly, but *why?*

In researching articles on teenage girls, I found many that discussed what is "wrong" with them, but thankfully, I also stumbled upon an article that a teenage girl wrote for her North Allegheny Senior High School newspaper, *The Uproar*, in Pennsylvania. Michelle Hwang highlights in her piece titled "The Power of Teenage Girls" how the love of teenage girls is responsible for launching the extraordinary success of the Beatles. Beatlemania stemmed from girls' love-filled enthusiasm, and Hwang points out:

"Perhaps teenage girls get overly excited about the little things. And maybe we do walk through life with our senses turned up. But this ability to see and feel everything more intensely is a strength, not a weakness. Just because we shriek and cry when we see our favorite musicians does not make them any less of an artist. Society's flighty perception of us does not make our hobbies and our passions any less valid. And it certainly does not render our thoughts and our words insignificant. Because as Malala Yousafzai, Greta Thunberg, Mary Shelley, and the Beatles fans of the 60s show, our voices and our actions have the ability to start revolutions. And we deserve your respect."[11]

Yes!!! (with three exclamation points).

Revolutions indeed. In September 2022, the teenage girls of Iran ignited a revolution for their human rights. When 22-year-old Mahsa Amini was arrested for wearing an "improper" hijab and subsequently killed by the Islamic Republic's morality police, the women of Iran unleashed a reckoning in the schools and streets of the country.

During these protests, I spoke with an Iranian friend who lives there, who told me, "'The teenage girls here are braver than you could ever imagine. I consider them the leaders of the Women, Life, Freedom protest movement, and they're risking their lives in the way they're using their voices to fight for change."

Eighteen-year-old Celeste is Iranian and has been following the movement closely because she still has so many friends and family there. She shared with me, "These teenage girls, these leaders of the movement in Iran, want to break the cycle. They want to make sure that generations after them have more freedom and choices in their life. People are scared of a teenage girl stepping into her power . . . people are scared of her potential. She has tools at her disposal like emotional intelligence that can be overlooked, but they're incredibly powerful."

This pushes me to ask, *Can teenage girls guide us toward a new type of power, a new type of leadership, and a new way of being in this world?*

Particularly, I see teenage girls inspire a new world when they powerfully take their pain and turn it into purpose. When the world hurts them, instead of responding with violence, they figure out how they can create change.

In seeking healing during the difficult aftermath of her rape, Harper pursued mental health resources at her college that helped her so much that she started volunteering to help other students with their traumatic experiences. She now runs a support group for survivors of sexual violence and coleads a mental health coalition on campus. She's a leader, courageously centered on love.

When a teenage girl feels like she can make a difference, when she feels like her voice will matter and people will listen, then her greatest power unfolds. It's not selfish, not dominating, not oppressive, and not violent. This power has a large amount of self-efficacy, which is simply defined as the belief in your ability to succeed. It's intrinsic and not forced upon her. No amount of criticizing or controlling her choices will get her to this powerful place. She finds it for herself.

I turn back to the moments of a teenage girl running for school president. In her fear, what I've often seen happen is that a parent steps in to help. Making the posters, editing her speech, and just getting way too involved. I know parents are scared that she might not win, and I get it, because I'm also guilty of over-helping a girl with her school presidential campaign. No one wants to see a girl strive for leadership and fail. However, she needs to own the journey. She needs to find her own voice—not use the voice of what's worked in the past. Maybe she has a better way of doing it.

When we try to control or change a teenage girl, it limits her powerful potential. It limits an authentic exchange of love, because it inherently implies that who she is isn't good enough. Implying that someone should change sends the message that they need to be that way in order to earn or deserve love, *which isn't love*. When I was giving way too much advice on what a girl should put in her speech, she was internalizing *My idea isn't good, therefore I'm not good enough*. Instead, I could give her a ton of loving encouragement and ask, "What do you think?"

I've found that when I choose to love a teenage girl exactly as she is, without trying to change or control her, then it helps ignite this power deep within her soul. A power this world desperately needs. When Naomi lost the election for class president in seventh grade, she didn't give up. She tried again her senior year and was elected as the entire school's student body president. These girls don't want to give up. And when I'm comforting them in those times of loss, I've found that one piece of encouragement always lights up their heart:

The only way to guarantee failure *is to never try*.

In her essay "Love as the Practice of Freedom," bell hooks describes how the "moment we choose to love we begin to move against domination, against oppression. The moment we choose to love we begin to move towards freedom, to act in ways that liberate ourselves and others."[12]

In order for teenage girls to step into their power, there must be liberation from the systems that have held them back. We are all part of that system, and we all must choose our next step forward. Do you want to try to build a powerful new world that's based on love? Or do you want to continue to do it the same way we always have? The choice is yours.

**CORE INSIGHTS**

Power is not controlling or imposing your thoughts on others but letting yourself learn and be vulnerable. Doing that creates communication, then connection, and then community, which is power. The most powerful people I know are connecting to other people and lifting them up. —KAT, AGE 18

---

✦ Teenage girls believe we need to redefine *power*, steering us away from the limiting concepts of power that are characterized by domination, oppression, ego, wealth, physical power, violence, and self-interest.

✦ When a teenage girl feels like she can make a difference, like her voice will matter and people will listen, then she steps into a power that can transform the world.

✦ Girls characterize women's leadership as more peaceful, equal, cooperative, empathetic, communicative, fair, joyful, optimistic, and kind, which is the type of world they hope for.

✦ By combining care and courage, teenage girls reveal that the most powerful way to create something new and better in this world is through love.

✦ Loving teenage girls exactly as they are will help them step into their power.

CONCLUSION

# (LIBERATION)

*Let us live so we do not regret years of inertia and ignorance,*
*so when we die we can say all of our energy was dedicated to the*
*noble liberation of the human mind and spirit, beginning with my own.*[1]
—Maya Angelou

Connecting to powerful, wise, and angsty teenage girls has helped me find my truth and liberate the silenced, trapped voice inside of me. Each lesson that I learned, every struggle along the way, helped me see through the eyes of collective liberation. The idea that if we heal ourselves, we heal the world.

That said, we can be really resistant to change. It can feel safer to stick with what we know, even when we know it's not working. We need to look inside ourselves to ignite change, to take responsibility and do whatever we can to liberate ourselves.

Liberation is closely tied to every lesson in this book. Since the girls whose stories and thoughts fill these pages vary a lot by race, religion, ability, sexuality, and socioeconomic status, I thought that a discussion on liberation might specifically bring up injustices that affect them personally. But when I asked what *liberation* means to them, a wider scope appeared among their answers that was fascinatingly similar.

Bella told me, "Liberation acknowledges the larger system holding us back but that would free us to make our own choices."

Madelyn said, "Liberation is an internal battle because you're liberating your heart and mind from everything that's been pushed on you."

Juliette shared, "I'd feel liberated if there were no rules on how I *should* be or what I *should* do, then I would feel happy and like I could be myself."

Davina told me, "Liberation is realizing what's important to you and realizing that it doesn't need to be important to anyone else."

Fatima declared, "Liberation would be freedom from expectations. The freedom to explore myself, the real me."

Giselle shared, "Liberation means not being controlled in any way, and you just do what makes you happy."

Shanaya said, "Liberation is being able to be myself. Think my own thoughts, free from society's expectations."

They are all acknowledging something bigger that is holding them back, and all they want is to simply be themselves.

As much as I would love this book to completely uproot and dismantle the world's broken systems that have squashed, controlled, and feared teenage girls, all I can do is point the finger at myself. It's the only thing in my power. I can control my own choices. I can absorb the lessons that teenage girls have given me and try to create positive change however I can.

Knowing how much teenage girls have helped me, I'm hoping and asking if we can be there for them now too. If you've read something in this book and thought, "Oh no, I messed that up," that's totally okay and normal. I know that parents deeply want to do right by their daughters. I know that, in general, people want this world to be a positive place for girls.

One way that I've tried to take responsibility is by making amends. I'm not talking about the "sorrys" of people-pleasing. Those are just a flurry of words that are more about an appearance of likability and soothing my own discomfort. Girls can tell the difference. I'm talking about amends for when I do things like not listen to her, try to fix or minimize her feelings, put pressure on her, tell her what to do, or make assumptions. I own it, acknowledge it, and say I'm sorry.

Sometimes, I hesitate because I think maybe it wasn't a big deal or she didn't notice. But really, *teenage girls notice everything*. As they said from the beginning:

"We're a lot smarter than you think we are."

So, I choose to honor that wisdom by being real with them. That means I own my mistakes, make amends, and bring awareness around the behavior so I don't repeat it. Girls have told me that this type of "sorry" has made them feel seen, respected, and cared for. It also felt, for both of us, *liberating*. We don't have to be tied to old stories and old harm. Amends wipe the slate clean, so we can connect more vulnerably and honestly. It's really hard to improve and deepen a relationship without the liberating feeling of a clean slate. I'm trying to offer an option that can reset everything.

And now if you're like, *Really? I just read this whole book and the last takeaway is that I'm supposed to say "sorry" to my daughter?* Well, handing the microphone to the girls one last time, this is what they had to say when I asked what it would feel like to have their parents make amends.

Lucia told me, "I can barely imagine it, because it would never happen, but I feel like I would cry. If my parents were to apologize, I would finally be able to take a deep breath, go to sleep for a week, and wake up feeling so much better. We're put through so much and for what? There are so many expectations, so many rules that we need to follow. I just want to rest."

Izzy said, "Oh wow. First, I would feel shocked. I would actually wonder if they truly mean what they're saying because I wouldn't believe it's happening. It's hard for me to even think about or know what I'd feel because I'm never going to get an apology. But I know I would feel so relieved."

Marli shared, "It would be very freeing, like *finally* . . . I've been carrying the weight of the world trying to get their approval, and now they're acknowledging that it's been too much. But for them to realize the impact they've had on my mental health, they would have to be going through a life-changing moment themselves. I wouldn't believe it unless their behavior changed too."

Harper answered, "For one, that would never happen, but if they had ever chosen to apologize to me while growing up, it would have modeled healthier relationships for me. Instead, I've gotten into so many unhealthy relationships, and I've had to learn the hard way."

Riley told me, "My dad has never apologized to me for anything. It's actually all I want from him. I know we'll never work through everything, but an apology would heal those things that we may never talk through. If he were to apologize and recognize his role, I would feel so much better, rather than feeling like I have to forget in order to move on."

Zandy described, "It's more than them saying sorry, it's more about them seeing why they feel an apology is necessary. I honestly don't know what it would feel like, and this might sound sad, but I'm trying to live my life in a way that doesn't need an apology. They don't apologize because they're not ready and maybe they never will be."

Keisha told me, "I don't know if this makes sense, but if they apologized, it would make me feel heard. Because if you think I deserve an apology, then you know you did something wrong. But right now, I'm living in a world where adults think they've never done anything wrong."

Brianna said, "An apology would make me feel understood and appreciated and loved."

I didn't expect to write about amends in this conclusion, but after listening to girls share over and over again about needing this type of healing, it felt necessary. There is a lot of research to support the positive impact of what is often called "repair" in the psychology field. Studies show that the primary outcome of repair is trust.[2] Making amends repairs and builds trust. Emotional trust builds love. It also teaches a girl what it looks like to be a loving, healthy adult.

I was continually gutted by the girls' responses when I asked if they wanted or needed an apology from their parents, but thankfully there was some light.

Waverly shared with me, "I used to say I had the worst parents, and then we all went to therapy and learned how to apologize. Once they started listening to me and acknowledging their actions, it made us so much closer. It was so healing and I started to feel really safe in our relationship. I also feel safer to acknowledge my own mistakes because I feel like they're not judging me. Now when my parents apologize, we end up having a two-hour bonding talk, and I feel heard and loved."

Waverly is offering a hopeful vision, a world filled with more healing and love. If you have a teenage girl in your life who you would like to build love and trust with, I recommend making amends. Her heart and your heart will both expand in unexpected ways. You might know a specific instance that you can apologize for, but it could also be a quiet moment in the car together where you simply say:

"Hey, I wanted to say I'm sorry for not always hearing you. I haven't always been the best listener. I really want to start listening to you better. Is there a way I can make amends, something I can do that will make you feel more heard and understood?"

In moments like these, I hope you can be radically honest, own your mistakes, and share your imperfect humanness. She will respect it. And if you do it sincerely, she will probably cry tears of relief. Those grateful tears will be healing, let the feelings flow. And if she has a suggestion for changed behavior or she needs an additional sorry for something specific, please *please* listen and really try to give her what she needs. Don't get defensive. *Defensiveness doesn't heal anything.*

A clean slate will be hard if she doesn't truly believe that your dynamic will change. If you are yearning for a clean slate with her, then you can ask her directly after the apology:

"I would really love to have a clean slate with you. What would help make that possible?"

And for everyone, whether you have a teenage girl in your life or not, making amends transforms relationships into something more loving. Everyone wants to feel more heard and understood. Connecting to the wisdom of teenage girls has simply shown me the way forward. Their struggles shine a light on how we all can do better.

This world is not a friendly place for a teenage girl, but she's doing the best she can. I'm wholeheartedly hoping that we can choose to help her by giving her some freedom and some space to be herself.

Space for her feelings. Space for her choices. Space for her sexuality. Space to mess up. Space to be angry. Space to be imperfect. Space away from expectations. Space to find her own beauty. Space to explore her identity. Space to tell her radical truth. Space to use her voice. Space to share her insecurities and fears. Space to be seen, heard, and understood. And space to be the loving force that she already is.

This space is *liberating* for her, and it will create room for her full power to unfold. It'll be like watching a sunset, but not a simple horizon sunset.

I've always found that a clean horizon sunset with the backdrop of a clear blue sky is boring. However, a sunset with scattered clouds can turn the sky into the most epic and stunning artistry of colors, creating pinks, oranges, reds, purples, blues, and yellows, painting the sky with the spirit of ever-changing, unfettered creativity.

When people try to force someone down the path of robotically pursuing likability and "perfection," I see a boring horizon sunset that's not living its full potential. It's the same muted flute not sharing its feelings. It's the superficial compliments and a people-pleasing "I'm fine." It's the person who can't handle my mess, who can't handle the clouds in my sky, so I hide them in shame, not letting myself feel truly seen and understood.

Fear takes hold and a boring blue-sky sunset just feels "safer." I manipulate myself into what I think people want: a life without clouds. But in reality, there are clouds in a person's life. I've named the "clouds" a lot of different things in this book:

A mud pool of mistakes, unpleasant feelings, insecurity, a mess, secrets, "flaws," self-doubt . . . all the things that make us human.

I've had to confront the clouds, which wouldn't have been possible without people supporting me with a great deal of love—a liberating type of love. A love that doesn't judge.

I'm asking, What would the world look like if we stopped judging teenage girls and simply loved them in a way that embraced their clouds and allowed them to step into their completely liberated power? That fearless sunset would set the sky on fire.

I believe that this new reality would help liberate all of us. But we'd have to let go of what we're clinging to—the fear, perfectionism, shame, emotional walls, societal rules, lying, judgment, and attempts to control.

Teenage girls often have an attitude of *burn it all down*. I used to think this nihilistic mentality didn't offer any hope. However, in better understanding their needs and vision for the future, I now see this desire as revolutionary. It's not an attitude of destruction, but an attitude of creativity that deeply yearns for a blank canvas.

They envision a revolution where we collectively create something braver, something authentic, something free, and something filled with love. I'm inviting you to step into that unknown with me. Please don't underestimate the beautiful potential, because I've learned from the wisdom of teenage girls that there's a source of power and love there that's beyond our wildest expectations.

## ACKNOWLEDGMENTS

Gratitude is one of the most important practices of my entire life. My parents profoundly expanded my life by teaching me the significance of two simple words: Thank you.

This book wouldn't exist without the people I name here. **And if my heart were to ever explode from love, this is where you'll be able to find the cause for the explosion.**

**To all the girls who changed my life:** Mariasha Williams, Elizabeth Korbatov, Jaya Harper, Elissa and Ali Markowitz, Emmi Moelleken, Coco Cooley, Violet Hume Leitch, Scarlett and Tullah McColl, Ava Eisendrath, Elle Wisnicki, Chloe and Ally Steinfeld, Diane Orozco, Addy Fortener, Lila and Daria Mundy, Stella Raimondi, Setareh Kargahi, Lili and Emma Bernstein, Dami Ogundimu, Franki Brown, Nevaeh Moffatt, Athena Kurlak, Charley Siegel, Maddie Merle, Elliotte Puro, Rocio Orozco, Thea and Cy Larks, Samantha Kyle, Teagan O'Day, Sabrina Chatlani, Gianna Iacone, and so many more, but it's impossible to name all of you. . . . Thank you for trusting me. You're perfect exactly the way you are. With infinite love, I will be on your team forever, fighting for your voice to be heard.

**To my mom, Donna Dailey:** Thank you for boldly and lovingly supporting my uniqueness, which has helped me live a life of authenticity.

By guiding me to volunteer at a young age, you inspired me to also live a life of generosity, which has led me to this moment. Thank you for trusting me to make smart choices and helping me feel free and brave enough to make them.

**To my dad, Robin Dailey:** The way you have always loved me and believed in me has given me the courage to speak my truth in the world. Since I was little, you created tons of space for my voice to be heard, which profoundly helped me step into my power. You taught me to always show up for the people I love, with enthusiasm. Thank you for deeply understanding and supporting my dreams of a big life and never underestimating me.

**To my husband, Charles Goodan:** Thank you for always listening to me with so much love, inspiring me with fun and community, comforting me through all the anxious moments, cheering me on with absolute belief in my success, and being the most thoughtful person in my life. I will never be able to describe how much I love you.

**To my two nieces, Junia Dailey and Lemon Kerr:** In so many ways, this book is for you. I will never stop working to create a world where your voice will be heard and where you can be your most powerful and authentic self.

**To my amazing immediate family:** Erik Dailey; Phillip, Nadene, and Rémy Jacquet; Pamela Dailey; Colin, Molly, and Tom Waters; Kris and Roger Goodan; Margot, Sean, and Waylon Kerr; and my sister-in-law, Millason Dailey, who served as my chosen family representative to read drafts of this book: Thank you all for giving me so much love and support through so many years of growth and uncertainty. You mean so much to me.

**To my editor, Pamela Cannon:** Our collaboration was meant to be. Your powerful insights and support inspired the absolute best in me. You are an extraordinary force for good. I'll never forget how much you advocated for my voice and the vision of this book with your whole heart. Thank you for fiercely believing in a world where girls can step into their full power.

**To the world-class team at Gallery Books and Simon & Schuster,** specifically Jennifer Bergstrom, Sally Marvin, Jill Siegel, Mackenzie Hickey, Tyrinne Lewis, Aimee Bell, Kim Laws, Lisa Litwack, Davina Mock-Maniscalco, Sarah Wright, Dominick Montalto, and the amazing Sierra Fang-Horvath: The way you've championed this book with heartfelt enthusiasm has had a life-changing effect on me. With every detail, big or small, I have felt your genuine care. Are there awards for publishing teams? If so, you should WIN ALL OF THEM.

**To my agent, Karen Murgolo:** I didn't know literary agencies could be as wonderful as Aevitas, and there's absolutely no way I could have dreamed up a better agent than you. You've truly wowed me with your integrity. I could not have gotten through this without you. Your thoughtfulness and care make me feel like I can accomplish anything, and I'm beyond grateful to have you by my side.

**To my best friend, Bailey Conway Anglewicz:** No one is better than you at helping me process all of life's ups and downs. You've been there for not only the celebrations but also every struggle, and your wisdom has carried me through it all. I can't imagine doing life without you.

**To my best friend, Geoffrey Lind:** You're my radical honesty safe haven, where I'm humbly grounded, fully myself, and always laughing. You're my ride-or-die, and thankfully, we'll always have a place at the Dairy Queen.

**To Neil Strauss:** When I walked up to you over a decade ago and said that we were destined to be friends, I really had no idea how special our friendship would be. You've been an enlightening surprise in my life. Thank you for not only generously supporting me through this book journey but also for guiding me to be a writer who seeks creativity, vulnerability, personal growth, and purpose.

**To all of the incredible parents I've worked with:** Thank you for trusting me. Your kids are truly extraordinary. Specific gratitude goes to Jennifer Levin, Moon Zappa, Laura Dern, Jenni Konner, Jaclyn and Ben Harper, Gail Lyon, Nilou Panahpour, Chris Mundy, Jennifer and Andrew Bernstein, and Kirsty Hume for giving insights, support, notes, and testimonials that helped bring this moment to fruition.

**To my PR team, Jessica Jonap and Aileen Boyle:** You took a woman with no platform and believed her voice should be heard on every platform. I'm so grateful for everything you do.

**To Andrea Prince:** I wouldn't be here without you. Thanks to the divine plan, not my plan.

**To Emily Morse, Samara Bay, and Liz Plank:** Thank you for believing in this book from the very beginning, generously offering your help. Whether you were passing along a pitch to your agent or giving me brilliant author insights, you've most of all been my soul-friend who elevates me, because you're so inspiring.

**To Rebecca Quin/Becky Lynch:** Thank you for being the first person to read the entire first draft of the book, bolstering my resolve at a critical moment. Our friendship is also a result of me choosing to write this book, and for that, I will always be grateful.

**To the extraordinary humans Falguni Lakhani Adams, Danielle Aufiero, Jett Doucette Zappa, Emily Deschanel, Tara Schuster, Ivy Kwong, Les Hilger III, and the Writers' Roundtable:** Thank you for giving really smart notes on early drafts or offering strategic help, talking me through difficult moments, and encouraging me when I needed it most.

**To Pamela Madsen, Cosmo Meens, Court Vox, Christie Bemis, and Brittney King:** Thank you for helping me discover and liberate my own creative power, helping me become the woman who could write this book.

**To the phenomenal friends Barbara Fiorentino, Pete Huyck, Dione Spiteri, Moby, Alex Cooley, Olivia and Will Forte, Kristi Korzec, Alison Eakle, and Milana Vayntrub:** Thank you for giving me specific encouragement and support at very specific moments in life that truly helped me believe in myself.

**And to all of my friends:** You have lit up my life with SO MUCH laughter and goodness. Thank you for keeping me centered on love.

There are so many more people I wish I could name, you know who you are.

**To my therapists, Terese Forster and Robyn Smith:** Thank you for being an integral part of my healing and evolution.

**To women in my life who have up-leveled my fight for gender justice: Jen Siebel Newsom, Eve Rodsky, Caroline Heldman, Suzanne Lerner, Sarah Jones, Janna Meyrowitz Turner, Dr. Maria Uloko, and Natasha Halevi:** Thank you for inspiring me to be even bolder.

**To Shauna Robertson, Magela Crosignani, Matty Libatique, Elizabeth Raposo, Darren Aronofsky, and Eric Watson:** Thank you for believing in me when I was so very young and welcoming me into creative spaces that expanded the course of my life.

**To DemocraShe's Sarah Jakle and Jessica Stamen:** Thank you for being my galvanizing teammates, working so hard to give tools and opportunities to teenage girls, so that they can be our future leaders. I'm better for knowing you and witnessing your remarkable impact. Our collaboration has inspired me beyond what I could have imagined.

**To Tony Porter, Ted Bunch, and everyone at the nonprofit A Call to Men:** Thank you for being a part of my soul-journey to better this world. The work we do together brings so much meaning and purpose to my life, and I'm eternally grateful for how you've never underestimated my ability and vision to inspire change.

**And lastly, to my high school drama teacher, Jodi Papproth:** When I was a teenage girl, you were the non-parent adult who sought to understand me, always listened, never judged, helped me discover my quirky authentic self, and let me be me. Thank you.

**I acknowledge all of these people with a heart that's very close to exploding because it's filled with *so much love*.**

# FEELINGS WHEEL

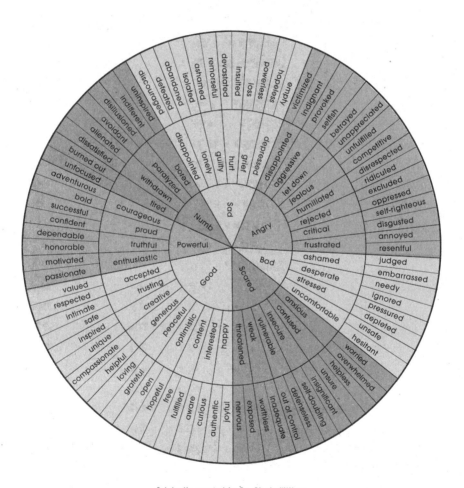

Originally created by Dr. Gloria Willcox

# EXPANDING CONVERSATIONS WITH TEENAGE GIRLS (OR ANY HUMAN BEING)

B elow are questions and comments that seek to understand and empower.

With all of these options, it's absolutely vital to have a judgment-free tone that has no agenda and expresses genuine curiosity.

## TO UNDERSTAND:

+ What are your thoughts on that?

+ How do you feel about that?

+ Do you believe that?

+ How can I support you with that?

+ What do you need right now? Do you need me to just listen?

+ Do you want my thoughts or help on this?

+ Do you need some space?

+ Is there anything else you want to share about this?

✦ What do you actually like doing with your time?

✦ What do you wish you could do more of?

✦ What kind of change do you want to create in the world?

✦ What type of unfairness makes you sad or angry?

✦ Do you feel pressure to be perfect or likable?

✦ Do you feel like you need to please people around you?

✦ Do you feel like I listen to you enough?

✦ Do you feel heard and understood by me? If not, how could I improve?

✦ Do you think that I create an environment where it feels safe to tell the truth? Are there ways that I could be better at that?

✦ Are there ways that I could be more honest with you?

✦ Where do you think the voice of self-doubt comes from?

✦ What social media accounts have been inspiring you lately?

✦ Do you feel like you have a healthy relationship with social media?

✦ What does beauty mean to you?

✦ What do you think movies and TV are telling the world about sexuality and beauty?

✦ Do you feel like you can be totally yourself? If not, what types of things are holding you back?

✦ If the world had a majority of women leaders, how do you think it would be different?

✦ Do you feel like you can speak up when you disagree with me?

+ Do you think your voice is powerful?

+ I want to hear your perspective on this. Can I ask you more questions about it?

+ Why is this important to you? Tell me more.

+ I don't have an agenda here, I really just want to understand better.

## TO EMPOWER:

+ What do you think the solution is?

+ How would you like to handle this?

+ What do you want?

+ Is there anything you want to do about it?

+ What do you think the first step is?

+ What is your inner voice telling you? What does your gut say?

+ What choice feels right for you?

+ Without worrying about pleasing or disappointing people, what feels like the best course forward?

## AFTER *LISTENING* TO RESPONSES:
## I'M HEARING YOU SAY _____.
## AM I GETTING THAT RIGHT?

+ I really respect your thoughts on this.

+ I love hearing what you have to say.

- ✦ These are really smart thoughts.

- ✦ I trust your ability to make this decision.

- ✦ I'll let you handle it then.

- ✦ I'll support whatever you think is best.

- ✦ That's a great idea, better than my idea.

- ✦ You really inspire me.

- ✦ Sounds like you know what to do.

- ✦ That sounds like a really smart choice.

- ✦ I trust your judgment.

- ✦ I believe you.

- ✦ You have nothing to prove to me.

# NOTES

**BOOK EPIGRAPH**

1. Kelsey Sutton, *The Lonely Ones* (Toronto: Penguin Random House Canada, 2016).

**CHAPTER ONE: FEELINGS**

1. Pema Chödrön, *When Things Fall Apart: Heart Advice for Difficult Times* (Boston: Shambhala, 1996).
2. Sally C. Curtin, M.A., "State Suicide Rates Among Adolescents and Young Adults Aged 10–24, United States, 2000–2018," *National Vital Statistics Reports*, Volume 69, Number 11, September 11, 2020, https://www.cdc.gov/nchs/data/nvsr/nvsr69/nvsr-69-11-508.pdf.
3. Charlotte Johnson, M.A., LPCC, "Did You Know that Most Emotions Last 90 Seconds? Emotions Come and Go; However, Feelings Can Last a Long Time!" Care Counseling, https://care-clinics.com/did-you-know-that-most-emotions-last-90-seconds/.
4. Angelo Compare, Cristina Zarbo, Edo Shonin, William Van Gordon, and Chiara Marconi, "Emotional Regulation and Depression: A Potential Mediator between Heart and Mind," *Cardiovascular Psychiatry and Neurology*, June 22, 2014, https://www.ncbi.nlm.nih.gov/pmc/articles/PMC4090567/.

**CHAPTER TWO: CHOICE**

1. Thornton Wilder, *The Ides of March* (New York: HarperCollins, 2020).

## CHAPTER THREE: SEXUALITY

1. adrienne maree brown, *Pleasure Activism: The Politics of Feeling Good* (Chico, CA: AK Press, 2019).

2. "Sex and HIV Education," Guttmacher Institute, https://www .guttmacher.org/state-policy/explore/sex-and-hiv-education#:~:text =38%20states%20and%20the%20District,education%20and%2 For%20HIV%20education.

3. "U.S. Teen Girls Experiencing Increased Sadness and Violence," CDC Newsroom, February 13, 2023, https://www.cdc.gov/media /releases/2023/p0213-yrbs.html.

4. A Call to Men: The Next Generation of Manhood, https://www .acalltomen.org/.

5. Peggy Orenstein, *Girls & Sex: Navigating the Complicated New Landscape* (New York: HarperCollins, 2016).

6. Emily Morse, *Smart Sex: How to Boost Your Sex IQ and Own Your Pleasure* (New York: HarperCollins, 2023).


## CHAPTER FOUR: PERFECTION

1. Brené Brown, *The Gifts of Imperfection: Let Go of Who You Think You're Supposed to Be and Embrace Who You Are* (Center City, MN: Hazelden Publishing, 2010).

2. "Anxiety Disorders, Their Prevalence and Data Sources," National Institutes of Mental Health, https://www.nimh.nih.gov/health/statistics /any-anxiety-disorder.

3. "Stress in America: Are Teens Adopting Adults' Stress Habits?" American Psychological Association, February 11, 2014, https://www.apa .org/news/press/releases/stress/2013/stress-report.pdf.

4. "The Confidence Collapse and Why It Matters for the Next Generation," Ypulse, 2018, https://confidencecodegirls.com/poll.

5. Michele Cohen Marill, "Binge Eating Disorder," WebMD, October 13, 2021, https://www.webmd.com/mental-health/eating-disorders/binge -eating-disorder/binge-eating-disorder-medref#:~:text=The%20

findings%20show%20anorexia%20to,and%202.1%2Dfold%20 in%20females.

6. Stanford Medicine's Center for Compassion and Altruism Research and Education, "Self-Compassion," 2022, http://ccare.stanford.edu /research/wiki/compassion-definitions/self-compassion/.

7. Dr. Kristin Neff, "Test How Self-Compassionate You Are," Self -compassion.org, https://self-compassion.org/self-compassion-test/.

### CHAPTER FIVE: PEOPLE-PLEASING

1. Simi Horwitz, "Eve Ensler's Jewish Dialogue," *Forward*, December 11, 2012, https://forward.com/culture/167255/eve-enslers-jewish-dialogue/.

2. "Pressure & Perfectionism," Heart of Leadership, https://heartofleader ship.org/statistics/.

3. "The Confidence Collapse and Why It Matters for the Next Generation," Ypulse, 2018, https://confidencecodegirls.com/poll.

### CHAPTER SIX: COMPLIMENTS

1. Erica Boothby, Xuan Zhao, and Vanessa Bohns, "A Simple Compliment Can Make a Big Difference," *Harvard Business Review*, February 24, 2021, https://hbr.org/2021/02/a-simple-compliment-can-make-a -big-difference.

### CHAPTER SEVEN: RADICAL HONESTY

1. Audre Lorde, *Sister Outsiders: Essays and Speeches* (Feasterville-Trevose, PA: Crossing Press, 1984).

2. "Speak Truth to Power," Dictionary.com, August 14, 2020, https: //www.dictionary.com/e/slang/speak-truth-to-power/#:~:text=Rustin %20was%20a%20Black%20Quaker,is%20that%20war%20is%20 wrong.%E2%80%9D.

3. Lorde, *Sister Outsiders: Essays and Speeches*.

4. Howard Zinn, *Marx in Soho: A Play on History* (Cambridge, MA: South End Press, 1999).

## CHAPTER EIGHT: SELF-DOUBT

1. Oprah Winfrey, *What I Know for Sure* (New York: Macmillan, 2014).

2. "The Confidence Collapse and Why It Matters for the Next Generation," Ypulse, 2018, https://www.confidencecodegirls.com/poll.

3. "The Confidence Collapse," Ypulse, 2018.

4. "Media's Effect on Body Image," *Teen Health and the Media, Body Image & Nutrition*, Teen Futures Media Network, College of Education, University of Washington, https://depts.washington.edu/thmedia /view.cgi?page=fastfacts&section=bodyimage.

5. Taylor Swift, liner notes to *Fearless*, Big Machine Records, November 11, 2008.

6. Sukhman Rekhi, M.A., "Self-Acceptance: Definition, Quotes, & How to Practice It," Berkeley Well-Being Institute, https://www.berkeley wellbeing.com/self-acceptance.html.

7. Fabiane Frota da Rocha Morgado, Angela Nogueira Neves Betanho Campana, and Maria da Consolação Gomes Cunha Fernandes Tavares, "Development and Validation of the Self-Acceptance Scale for Persons with Early Blindness: The SAS-EB," *PLOS One*, September 30, 2014, https://www.ncbi.nlm.nih.gov/pmc/articles/PMC4182093/.

8. Dolly Parton, @DollyParton, "Find out who you are and do it on purpose," Twitter, April 8, 2015, https://twitter.com/DollyParton/status /585890099583397888?lang=en.

## CHAPTER NINE: FRIENDS

1. Joseph P. Lash, *Helen and Teacher: The Story of Helen Keller and Anne Sullivan Macy* (New York: Delacorte Press/Seymour Lawrence, 1980).

2. "Codependency," *Merriam-Webster Online Dictionary*, https://www .merriam-webster.com/dictionary/codependency.

3. Bep Uink, Kathryn Lynn Modecki, and Bonnie L. Barber, "Disadvantaged Youth Report Less Negative Emotion to Minor Stressors When with Peers: An Experience Sampling Study," *International Journal of Behavioral Development*, February 2016, DOI: 10.1177/0165025416 626516.

## CHAPTER TEN: THE MEDIA

1. Amanda Duberman, "Girl Power at the Peace Love & Misunderstanding Premiere," *Interview*, June 5, 2012, https://www.interviewmagazine.com/film/girl-power-at-the-peace-love-misunderstanding-premiere.

2. "Media & Eating Disorders," National Eating Disorders Association (NEDA), https://www.nationaleatingdisorders.org/media-eating-disorders.

3. "Study Shows Habitual Checking of Social Media May Impact Young Adolescents' Brain Development," University of North Carolina at Chapel Hill College of Arts and Sciences, January 3, 2023, https://www.unc.edu/posts/2023/01/03/study-shows-habitual-checking-of-social-media-may-impact-young-adolescents-brain-development/#:~:text=The%20study%20findings%20suggest%20that,more%20sensitive%20to%20social%20feedback.

4. Bechdel Test Movie List, https://bechdeltest.com/.

5. "Research Confirms that Black Girls Feel the Sting of Adultification Bias Identified in Earlier Georgetown Law Study," Georgetown Law Center on Poverty and Inequality, May 15, 2019, https://www.law.georgetown.edu/news/research-confirms-that-black-girls-feel-the-sting-of-adultification-bias-identified-in-earlier-georgetown-law-study/.

6. Stacy L. Smith, PhD, Marc Choueiti, and Katherine Pieper, PhD, "Inclusion or Invisibility? Comprehensive Annenberg Report on Diversity in Entertainment," Media, Diversity & Social Change, Institute for Diversity and Empowerment at Annenberg (IDEA), USC Annenberg School for Communication and Journalism, February 22, 2016, https://annenberg.usc.edu/sites/default/files/2017/04/07/MDSCI_CARD_Report_FINAL_Exec_Summary.pdf.

## CHAPTER ELEVEN: BEAUTY

1. Thich Nhat Hanh, *The Art of Power* (New York: HarperCollins, 2008).

2. "Eating Disorders Among Teen Girls," Eating Disorder Hope, https://www.eatingdisorderhope.com/risk-groups/eating-disorder-teen-girls.

3. "10 Statistics of Teenage Eating Disorders," Polaris Teen Center,

June 12, 2018, https://polaristeen.com/articles/10-statistics-of-teenage
-eating-disorders/.

4. "Survey Finds Disordered Eating Behaviors Among Three Out of Four American Women," *Carolina Public Health Magazine*, September 26, 2008, https://sph.unc.edu/cphm/carolina-public-health-magazine-accelerate-fall-2008/survey-finds-disordered-eating-behaviors-among-three-out-of-four-american-women-fall-2008/.

5. Jennifer L. Gaudiani, *Sick Enough: A Guide to the Medical Complications of Eating Disorders* (Oxfordshire, UK: Routledge, 2018).

6. Kelsey Miller, "Study: Most Girls Start Dieting by Age 8," *Refinery29*, January 26, 2015, https://www.refinery29.com/en-us/2015/01/81288/children-dieting-body-image.

7. Saint Augustine of Hippo, *Homilies on the First Epistle of John* (Hyde Park, NY: New City Press, 2008), https://www.newcitypress.com/homilies-on-the-first-epistle-of-john-study-edition.html.

8. Jean Anouilh, *Mademoiselle Colombe* (New York: Samuel French Inc. Plays, 1954), https://digitalcollections.nypl.org/items/510d47de-8b1e-a3d9-e040-e00a18064a99.

## CHAPTER TWELVE: IDENTITY

1. Oscar Wilde, *Oscar Wilde's The Portrait of Mr W H: "Be yourself; everyone else is already taken"* (London: Miniature Masterpieces, 2017).

2. "Where Does 'Impostor Syndrome' Come From?" *Merriam-Webster Online Dictionary*, https://www.merriam-webster.com/words-at-play/what-is-impostor-syndrome.

3. "KPMG Study Finds 75% of Female Executives Across Industries Have Experienced Imposter Syndrome in Their Careers," KPMG, October 7, 2021, https://info.kpmg.us/news-perspectives/people-culture/kpmg-study-finds-most-female-executives-experience-imposter-syndrome.html.

4. Ellen Friedrichs, "What Is the Average Age to Come Out?" liveabout dotcom, September 18, 2017, https://www.liveabout.com/what-is-the-average-age-to-come-out-1415428.

5. "U.S. Teen Girls Experiencing Increased Sadness and Violence," CDC Newsroom, February 13, 2023, https://www.cdc.gov/media /releases/2023/p0213-yrbs.html.

6. "Mental Health of Black Transgender and Nonbinary Young People," The Trevor Project, February 28, 2023, https://www.thetrevorproject .org/research-briefs/mental-health-of-black-transgender-and-non binary-young-people-feb-2023/.

7. "2022 National Survey on LGBTQ Youth Mental Health," The Trevor Project, https://www.thetrevorproject.org/survey-2022/.

8. "LGBTQ Youth Experiencing Homelessness," National Center for Homeless Education, https://nche.ed.gov/lgbtq-youth/.

9. Steve Jobs, Stanford University commencement speech, June 12, 2005, https://news.stanford.edu/2005/06/12/youve-got-find-love-jobs-says/.

10. Michelle Obama, *Becoming: A Guided Journal for Discovering Your Voice* (New York: Clarkson Potter, 2019).

11. Betty Friedan, *The Feminine Mystique* (New York: W.W. Norton, 1963).

## CHAPTER THIRTEEN: SHAME

1. Natalie Baker, "We're Only as Sick as Our Secrets," American Addiction Centers, January 4, 2022, https://recovery.org/were-only-as-sick -as-our-secrets/.

2. Korin Miller, "The Shocking Results of Yahoo Health's Body-Positivity Survey," *Yahoo!life*, January 4, 2016, https://www.yahoo.com/lifestyle /the-shocking-results-of-yahoo-1332510105509942.html?fr=yhssrp _catchall.

3. Sonali Kohli, "The Problem with Slut Shaming in Schools," *Los Angeles Times*, February 22, 2016, https://www.latimes.com/local/education /lausd/la-me-edu-slut-shaming-20160218-story.html.

4. Margot Goblet and Fabienne Glowacz, "Slut Shaming in Adolescence: A Violence Against Girls and Its Impact on Their Health," *International Journal of Environmental Research and Public Health*, June 21, 2021, https://www.ncbi.nlm.nih.gov/pmc/articles/PMC8296320/.

5. Kohli, "The Problem with Slut Shaming in Schools."

6. Sarah Epstein, LMFT, "What Is Both/And Thinking?" *Psychology Today*, February 23, 2021, https://www.psychologytoday.com/us/blog/between-the-generations/202102/what-is-bothand-thinking.

7. Catherine Cote, "Growth Mindset vs. Fixed Mindset: What's the Difference?" Harvard Business School Online, March 10, 2022, https://online.hbs.edu/blog/post/growth-mindset-vs-fixed-mindset#:~:text=Someone%20with%20a%20growth%20mindset,stable%20and%20unchangeable%20over%20time.

8. Brené Brown, *The Gifts of Imperfection: Let Go of Who You Think You're Supposed to Be and Embrace Who You Are* (Center City, MN: Hazelden Publishing, 2010).

9. Brown, *The Gifts of Imperfection*.

10. "Meet Tarana Burke, Activist Who Started 'Me Too' Campaign to Ignite Conversation on Sexual Assault," Democracy Now!, October 17, 2017, https://www.democracynow.org/2017/10/17/meet_tarana_burke_the _activist_who.

## CHAPTER FOURTEEN: POWER

1. Kathy Calvin, "Celebrating International Day of the Girl," United Nations Foundation, October 11, 2013, https://unfoundation.org/blog/post/celebrating-girls/.

2. Dacher Keltner, "The Power Paradox," *Greater Good Magazine*, December 1, 2007, https://greatergood.berkeley.edu/article/item/power _paradox.

3. bell hooks, *Ain't I a Woman: Black Women and Feminism* (Cambridge, MA: South End Press, 1982).

4. Liz Plank, *For the Love of Men: A New Vision for Mindful Masculinity* (New York: Macmillan, 2019).

5. bell hooks, *Feminism Is for Everybody: Passionate Politics* (London: Pluto Press, 2000).

6. "Facts and Figures: Women's Leadership and Political Participation," UN Women, https://www.unwomen.org/en/what-we-do/leadership -and-political-participation/facts-and-figures.

7. Emma Hinchliffe, "Women CEOs Run More Than 10% of Fortune 500 Companies for the First Time in History," *Fortune*, January 12, 2023, https://fortune.com/2023/01/12/fortune-500-companies-ceos-women-10-percent/.

8. "Feminism," *Cambridge Dictionary*, https://dictionary.cambridge.org/us/dictionary/english/feminism.

9. Mohadesa Najumi, "Why the Woman Who Does Not Require Validation from Anyone Is the Most Feared Individual on the Planet," *Huffington Post UK*, March 17, 2014, https://www.huffingtonpost.co.uk/mohadesa-najumi/ban-bossy-women-who-do-not-need-validation-are-feared_b_4971919.html.

10. adrienne maree brown, *Emergent Strategy: Shaping Change, Changing Worlds* (Chico, CA: AK Press, 2017).

11. Michelle Hwang, "The Power of Teenage Girls," *The Uproar*, April 22, 2021, https://nashuproar.org/44382/opinion/the-power-of-teenage-girls/.

12. bell hooks, "Love as the Practice of Freedom," published in *Outlaw Culture* (Oxfordshire, England: Routledge, 1994).

## CONCLUSION (LIBERATION)

1. Arthur Austen Douglas, *928 Maya Angelou Quotes* (Trumbull, CT: UBTech, 2016).

2. Fengling Ma, Breanne E. Wylie, Xianming Luo, Zhenfen He, Rong Jiang, Yuling Zhang, Fen Xu, and Angela D. Evans, "Apologies Repair Trust via Perceived Trustworthiness and Negative Emotions," *Frontiers in Psychology*, April 3, 2019, https://www.ncbi.nlm.nih.gov/pmc/articles/PMC6457316/.

Chelsey Goodan has been an academic tutor and mentor for 16 years, with a particular emphasis on the empowerment of teenage girls. She regularly speaks to audiences about gender justice, conducts workshops, and coaches parents on how to better understand and connect with their daughters. She is the founder of The Activist Cartel and the mentorship director of DemocraShe, a nonprofit that guides teenage girls from historically underrepresented communities into leadership positions. As an activist, she advises public figures, galvanizes volunteers, and organizes large-scale events for national nonprofits while also serving on the board of A Call to Men, a nonprofit working to end gender-based violence. Her passion to explore humanity's potential for authenticity, liberation, and empowerment permeates all of her work. A graduate of NYU's Tisch School of the Arts, Chelsey lives in Los Angeles.